Coursework Explained: Child Development

Valda Reynolds Cert. Ed.
Joint Chief Examiner, Midland Examining Group
for GCSE Home Economics: Child Development

Stanley Thornes (Publishers) Ltd.

Text © Valda Reynolds 1990

Original line illustrations © ST(P) Ltd. 1990

The copyright holders authorise ONLY purchasers of this book to make photocopies or stencil duplicates of charts and observation sheets on pages 10, 11, 12, 13, 19, 20, 22, 23, 27, 28, 33, 44, 55, 59, 61, for their own or their classes' immediate use within the teaching context.

No other rights are granted without permission in writing from the publisher or under licence from the Copyright Licensing Agency Limited. Further details of such licences (for reprographic reproduction) may be obtained from the Copyright Licensing Agency Limited, of 33–4 Alfred Place, London WC1E 7DP.

Copy by any other means or for any other purpose is strictly prohibited without the prior written consent of the copyright holders.

Applications for such permission should be addressed to the publishers: Stanley Thornes (Publishers) Ltd, Old Station Drive, Leckhampton, CHELTENHAM GL53 0DN, England.

First published in 1990 by:
Stanley Thornes (Publishers) Ltd.
Old Station Drive
Leckhampton
CHELTENHAM GL53 0DN
England

British Library Cataloguing in Publication Data

Reynolds, Valda
   Coursework explained: child development.
   1. Children. Development
   I. Title
   155.4

ISBN 0–7487–0177–X

Line artwork by Taurus Graphics, Abingdon, Oxfordshire.
Typeset by Tech-Set, Gateshead, Tyne & Wear.
Printed and bound in Great Britain at Ebenezer Baylis & Son Ltd, Worcester.

Contents

Using this book — v

Examination terms — vi

Introduction — x
   Coursework components — x
   General guidelines — xi

Component One – The observational study — 1
   Work Unit 1 – Preliminary Observational Exercises — 5
   Work Unit 2 – Observational Study: Mobility — 8
   Work Unit 3 – Group Observational Study: Socialisation Skills and Play — 15
   Work Unit 4 – Observational Study: Manipulative Skills and Creativity — 27
   Observational Study – further ideas — 31

Component Two – Practical items — 32
   Design Brief 1 – A wooden toy — 37
   Design Brief 2 – Soft furnishings for the nursery — 45
   Practical Items – further ideas — 50

Component Three – Investigative work — 53
   Investigation 1: Community Provision for the Under-Fives — 56
   Investigation 2: Clothing for the Baby and Child — 62
   Investigative Work – further ideas — 69

Syllabuses and past examination papers — 71

Video suppliers — 72

Index — 73

Acknowledgements

The author would like to thank the following people for their help and advice on this book:

Jean Marshall, Chief Moderator for the MEG Child Development GCSE Course; Staff Nurse Julie Payne and Derby County Special Care Baby Unit for information and providing a selection of premature baby clothes used in the photo on p. 63; Frances Price for the loan of children's toys and cot soft furnishings used in the photos on pp. xii and 49; Peter Reynolds for designing and making the wooden toy in Practical Item – Brief 1 and for his help with the index, word processing and checking of proofs.

The author and publisher are grateful to the following for permission to reproduce line artwork in this publication:

BBC Books Ltd. – *Making Toys* (1975) (p. 50)

NFER Nelson – *From Birth to Five Years* by Mary Sheridan (pp. 10–12)

The Open University – 'The First Year of Life': *Book 4 – The Developing Child* (pp. 10–12)

The author and publisher are grateful to the following for permission to reproduce photographs:

Early Learning Centre (p. 5, C1)
Graphique Photography (pp. 43, 49, 63)
Lupe Cunha (p. 5, A1, B1 & 2, C2, p. 17)
Mothercare UK Ltd. (p. 5, A2, pp. 45, 64, 67)
John Reynolds (p. xii)
Wizzywear Ltd. (p. 65)

Every effort has been made to contact copyright holders and we apologise if any have been overlooked.

Using this book

To the teacher

The initial difficulties associated with teacher assessed coursework have now largely been ironed out as teachers have become more experienced and confident. This book is for teacher support as well as to give guidance to pupils.

My aim has been to cover the coursework requirements for the six major GCSE examining boards, to look towards future developments in Technology to provide ground work for modular courses. I have given general and specific guidelines for each coursework component followed by actual (though not necessarily complete) examples to give your pupils some initial practice before they embark on the real thing, and these should help to stimulate their ideas. The photocopiable charts and observation sheets on pages 10, 11, 12, 13, 19, 20, 22, 23, 27, 28, 33, 44, 55, 59, 61, will help to develop observation skills and provide examples upon which pupils can base their own work. It is not intended that the work units should be used and entered by pupils as actual examination work.

To the pupil

Coursework is now a compulsory part of many examination syllabuses. In writing this book I have had to use accepted examination language, much of which seems difficult. Do not be put off by this; I have tried to help by explaining most of the terms in a glossary which you will find just after the contents page.

The book covers the three aspects of child development coursework found in the syllabuses of most of the examining groups. These are the observational study, the practical item and the investigative work. I have given guidelines and working examples to help stimulate your own ideas.

Coursework gives you an opportunity to study in depth parts of the syllabus which interest you. I hope you enjoy your coursework as much as I have enjoyed producing this sample material.

Examination terms

Accepted norms The level of development expected in a child at certain ages and stages of development
Achievement A standard of performance
Aims Purposes or goals behind your course of study. These are set out in the National Criteria and are common to all Home Economics courses
Analyse Break down into small parts and then study the results
Appropriate Suitable, fitting
Area of development An aspect of a child's growth
Assessment objectives These are a checklist of qualities which are set out at the beginning of every syllabus. They state exactly what the examiners will be awarding marks for. They are the same in all Home Economics courses and broadly cover: knowledge, understanding, evaluation.
Assignments Tasks to be done

Background information Collection of facts relating to the subject being studied
Bibliography List of books and written articles used
Brief (n) A short clear statement of what is going to be done

Category A group, section or collection
Characteristics Features which identify a person or thing
Checklist A list of things or activities to verify
Choice Restricted, a limited choice
Common elements The four aspects which make up Home Economics: Home, Food, Textiles, Family
Common themes The subjects which bring together the four aspects: health, interaction with environment, safety, human development, aesthetics, values, efficiency (HISHAVE)

Comparative record sheet A form which contrasts one child's achievements with another's
Component Part of a whole
Compulsory list Things which must be done
Conclusions Summing up
Content of the syllabus The subject matter to be studied
Coursework The work to be carried out during your course; it may be written or practical
Critical appraisal A judgement of the value of something

Developmental study An examination of a child's growth

Evaluation Making a study of what has been done, judging its value
Examination boards (groups) The bodies who draw up the syllabus, set and mark the work and award the grades
Expectations What you expect will happen

Forward planning Thinking something out in advance
Formulate To state clearly

Grade A mark awarded for the quality of your work
Graduated Progressed in stages
Guidance Help and direction given
Guidelines A set of helpful rules to follow

Identify To state what or how
Illustrative (material) Pictures, drawings etc. to explain your work
Investigation, investigative To search for information and make detailed enquiries

Justify To give reasons, to prove something

Manipulative (skills) To use the hands; practical skills
Manuals Handbooks for guidance
Mark allocation How marks are given
Mark weighting How marks are given to each part to show the level of importance
Marking scheme The answers to questions and the marks awarded
Modification Alteration

National criteria A set of rules, stating what the course should cover and how it should be assessed
Negative Lacking quality, having poor attitudes

Objectives Aims
Observational studies To look at something closely and write down what you see
Oral work Work done by talking and on tape

Positive Good, definite attitude
Practical skills Activities needing hand skills as well as thinking skills
Precise Exact and accurate
Preliminary planning To work out a plan in advance
Progressive observational study Following the progress made in a child's development over a period of time
Projects (topics) A piece of research work

Questionnaire A set of questions with a purpose

Record To write down the facts; to keep a written account
Relevant Bearing upon the matter being presented
Requirements Needs
Research Finding information from books etc. and then selecting and recording it
Resources Useful books, people, places for information gathering
Restricted selection A limited choice
Review Look back over your work

Social relationship Getting on with other people
Socialisation Mixing with other people
Study areas Parts into which your syllabus or work is divided
Subject content The areas of knowledge to be covered in that particular syllabus
Syllabus Information supplied by the examining groups, giving details of what you will need to study for a particular subject and how it will be examined

Time factor Length of time allowed
Topics (see **projects**)

Weightings Degree of importance attached, number of marks allowed

Introduction

Learning about babies, young children and family life is essentially a practical subject and the more practical experience you can get, the better your understanding will be. This is one reason why most Child Development courses have a high percentage of coursework. Coursework is also important to you because in many examination syllabuses a considerable proportion of marks is given to the practical aspect, sometimes as much as 60%. The other important factor is that your coursework should run throughout the full period of your course and will be constantly assessed by your teacher. All coursework is compulsory and sometimes failure to submit any one component may result in your not being awarded a grade.

Coursework components

The coursework required from the six main examining groups will be one, two or all three of the following components.

1 An observational study
This study of a child or children over a period of time can take the form of:
- a) a working note book,
- b) a folio or diary,
- c) a written record of observation, or
- d) an observational/developmental study.

2 Investigative work
You may have to do one or more *investigations* into various topics concerned with Child Development. Some boards give a free choice of topic, others give a range of topics or assignments to choose from.

3 An item to be made
This is usually a toy, game or garment for a child, perhaps linked to the child or children studied in the observational/developmental study, or a piece of practical work connected with the child.

The main purposes of these pieces of practical coursework are:
- a) to show that you have had some continuous experience with young children and are aware of their needs,
- b) to show that you can identify a problem or a need and put forward some possible solutions.

The following pages contain advice and suggestions for presenting your work. The work units are there for guidance; you will need to do the investigative work for yourself.

General guidelines

1 Understand the syllabus

You will need to know at the beginning of your course:
- what is in the syllabus i.e. what you will study
- how much coursework is required
- the skills which you must demonstrate
- the assessment objectives which are being tested in your coursework.
    These are given at the beginning of your syllabus and they test:
    knowledge and recall
    understanding and practical skills
    evaluation and values.
    Different syllabuses place different weightings on the assessment objectives.
- what the components are
- if you have freedom of choice or if the syllabus gives a restricted selection
- when each component must be finished and the date for handing it in.

Your teacher may give you an outline of the syllabus requirements and, because the terms used in the syllabus are very difficult, may simplify it for you. If you do not understand what is expected of you, ask questions until you do. Look at the Examination Terms at the beginning of the book which explain some of the terms used in the syllabus.

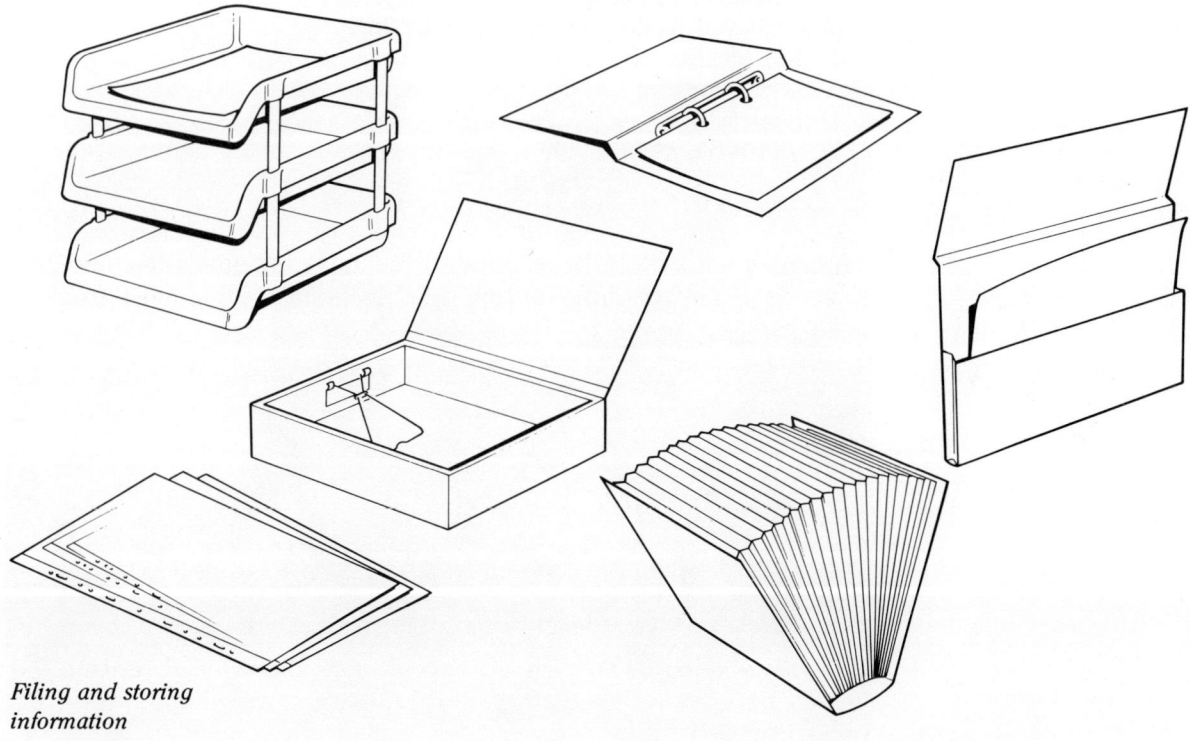

Filing and storing information

Introduction

2 Organisation

This is a very important skill. Do not jumble all your work together in a large box. Discover the various methods of filing and storing information, e.g.:

* plastic stacking trays
* manilla envelopes
* ring binders
* plastic wallets
* box files
* index boxes
* colour coded files.

Whichever you use, make sure your work is labelled. File research information such as newspaper and magazine cuttings, leaflets and instructions in separate containers for each topic. Place your topic work in its file as you finish it and keep it very safe and away from small children in your family or animals who could damage it.

3 Mark weighting and assessment

Find out how many marks are given for each piece of coursework. The child study, diary, folio or observational study which many courses require can carry a large proportion of the marks. It is only sensible, therefore, to spend more of your time on this than on a component such as an investigation, which may only carry half as many marks.

Your teacher should tell you how marks are allocated for each piece of coursework. It is important to realise that if you are to follow through the ideals of the GCSE examination, you must:
□ *identify* a need or problem
□ *investigate* and *apply* your knowledge to try to solve the problem
□ *decide* what to do and *plan* how to do it

This is an example of student's work

General guidelines

- show *how* you obtain your information and *justify* your choice of materials, design etc.
- use *practical skills* to produce a finished piece of work
- *record* each process as you go along
- *review* the success of your work, *assess* its strengths and weaknesses
- *decide* how your work could be improved, and devise ways of using your work in future projects.

The finished object is only a small part of the work to be assessed. You may produce a beautiful toy or garment for a child, such as those shown in the pictures, but if the supporting explanations are unclear or inadequate you will only achieve a low mark.

4 The Time Factor

As this will probably be only one of many of your examination subjects which has coursework components, you will need to plan your work carefully. You cannot leave them all until the final term of your examination course. Try to decide on a subject area, investigate a range of approaches and then develop your plan of work.

To be successful, you need to organise yourself.

∗ explore the area you are studying ∗ plan your work carefully ∗ follow through your planning ∗ finish a piece of work ∗ keep it somewhere very safe ∗ keep a continuous piece of work such as a child study, constantly up to date ∗ make up any work missed through illness as soon as possible ∗ a 'Year Planner' on your bedroom wall will help you to plan out your year's coursework and to keep to deadlines.

5 Choice of Work

This is a very important issue. First, you must work out what the syllabus requires you to do and then consider:

a) originality

Do choose a topic because:
you are interested in that topic
you know something about it
you can find out information about it
you have a special connection with the topic e.g. a family member with a particular handicap.

Do not choose a topic because:
your friend is doing it
it seems like an easy subject
you can't think of anything else.

b) level of skills

Do stretch yourself: something which is too easy will become boring and will not be very rewarding. Ask your teacher if you are not sure.

Do not choose to do something which is going to be too difficult for you or you will lose interest and have a poor result.

To choose a topic for your coursework, study the subject matter in your syllabus, select a theme that interests you, then narrow this theme down to give you a realistic choice which you can work with.

Before starting a piece of coursework you could have group discussions and 'brainstorming' sessions to stimulate ideas. Your teacher may also have suggestions, but remember, the final choice is yours.

6 Appearance and presentation

The appearance of your work is important. If it is neat, varied and orderly it will give a good impression. There are many ways of presenting information apart from long, written accounts which can become boring and repetitive. The method of presentation should suit the information being presented. Don't forget to give reasons to justify your selection of methods.

You could use:
- charts, diagrams, maps and graphs to present factual information
- pictures and photographs which add interest when well explained
- audio tapes for interviewing children, parents, social workers etc.
- video equipment to record a playgroup session, children's party, antenatal class.

When using audio/visual recorders, computers etc, seek help from your teacher. There should be simple instruction manuals.

Do not clutter your work with printed information from food manufacturers, voluntary societies, shop catalogues etc. Use and interpret the information and present it in your own way. Remember; what counts is quality, not quantity.

7 Resources

Once you have decided on an area of work for your coursework, begin looking for information. Many manufacturers and specialist shops are flooded with requests and cannot cope with them all. You can try:
- asking your teacher – she/he may have a stock of leaflets or booklets for reference
- asking expectant mothers or mothers with small children whom you know – they may have been given leaflets by the clinic
- visiting exhibitions such as those in museums, public libraries and local health authority displays.

Do not expect others to do your information-seeking for you.

8 Teacher guidance and other help

Your teacher is your best resource. She/he will guide you and show you where to go for further help. If you have chosen to do something too difficult for your level of skill, and your teacher has to give you lots of help, she will have to take this into account when awarding marks for your work. Some syllabuses give precise information about the number of marks to be deducted for teacher intervention, some leave it for the teacher to decide. Another source of help is the experience of your own family. Your parents, grandparents and other relations will all have had experience of bringing up children and may know about the help available from the community. Remember, however, that your parents must not do the work for you.

9 Grade achievement and expectations

GCSE spans a very wide range of achievement. Do not expect to get a top grade unless you have very high ability and have worked very hard. The examination is there to test what you have done and award marks for positive achievement. Coursework provides the opportunity for you to achieve a satisfactory standard by:

* using practical skills   * solving problems   * collecting and using information   * assessing results   * applying knowledge.

Just to learn facts and reassemble them is a negative method of learning.

Enjoy your coursework, become interested and don't let it become a burden. You will know a great deal more about pregnancy, babies, child development and family life by the time you have finished!

COMPONENT ONE
The observational study

Guidelines

The syllabus contains notes to guide you; these notes explain which parts are compulsory. You must be aware of the following points before you begin your study.

- The age of the child/children. This may be from conception to five, six or seven years. If the age of the child studied goes above that specified, the study may be unacceptable to the board.
- Whether one child is to be studied or a group of children: usually there is a choice.
- The length of the study: some syllabuses suggest a maximum number of words e.g. 2500 to 3000.
- The form which the study must take, e.g. a working notebook, a diary, a folio.
- The time suggested for studying the child/children. This may vary from six weeks to several months, but the length of the study period should give you sufficient time to observe the child/children closely and notice changes in development.
- The areas of development which you should study. You may be able to study the child as a whole, or you may need to choose one (or more) major area(s) of development, e.g. intellectual development, language development, creativity.
- A study of handicapped children is more difficult; if this is the type of child study you wish to do, check that the syllabus allows for it.
- Check the mark weighting of the study to judge what proportion of your time you should be giving to this component.
- The common elements (i.e. food, textiles, home) will need to be included in your study. Your syllabus may expect you to identify them clearly.

Confidentiality
Get permission from the child's parents before you start (written permission if possible). If it is a group of children at a nursery school or playgroup then your teacher will get permission for you.

Choose another name and address for your child, to use in your study, if the parents wish it or if it is suggested in your syllabus.

Treat confidential family details with sensitivity. The child's parents may wish to see the finished study and may resent personal details being included. Check with them first.

Dates
Always date your work carefully throughout and indicate clearly the child(ren)'s age at the beginning and end of the study. You should be making your observations of the child regularly over an extended period

of time, perhaps two or three times a week. Remember to date and write your reports soon after the observation period.

Oral work

Interviews and discussions can be an interesting part of your work and marks will be gained for them, but you must keep a record of your oral work. If your teacher discusses or questions you about your study she will record this so that it may be assessed.

Up to date information

The information which you research and investigate must be up to date and you must be aware of current ideas in the care and development of young children. You can then use this information by applying it to the child(ren) you are studying.

Marking scheme

The work which you must do for your study will be divided into several parts and each part allocated a proportion of the marks. Your teacher will explain this to you and it is useful to have a printed sheet of the mark breakdown. For the allocation of the marks your study may be broken into three broad areas.

	Mark Allocation Average range between the main exam groups
Area 1 Introduce and give background information about the child. Outline your plan and order of work. State the area(s) of development you have chosen and give reasons. Record your observations of the child, perhaps in the form of a diary. Relate your observations to the areas of development.	55%–63%
Area 2 Compare the results of your observations with current ideas to be found in books, magazines, TV. etc. Compare the child's results with those of other children in that age group.	13%–25%
Area 3 Evaluate: how effective was your planning? Were the methods you used successful and is the presentation good? What, if any, improvements could be made? How could your work be developed further?	20%–23%

Planning your observational study

Decisions

Before you begin there are several decisions you must make.
- Do you know an individual child and his/her family well enough to be able to complete an informative study? Will the parents give permission?
- Would you find it more convenient to study a *group* of children, i.e. at a playgroup or nursery school?

- Can you attend regularly, with your school's permission, at a playgroup, so that you can achieve a continuous, in-depth study?
- Which area(s) of development are you interested in? It is very difficult to do a study which involves 'general' development as this subject is very extensive and your study may become unfocused. See what your syllabus suggests. These are some examples:

   * creativity   * language development   * development through play   * environmental influences   * development of number concepts   * learning through play   * social interaction   * physical co-ordination

- How long will you study the child(ren); for several weeks or months?
- Which books and up-to-date materials will you use and where will you go to obtain resource material?
- What methods will you use to present your work in an interesting and organised way?

Now you must make a rough plan of what to include in your study. Follow the guidelines set out in the syllabus and the information from your teacher. You can adapt this plan as you go along, but do make sure that you have a checklist of what should be included, to tick off as you complete each item. Also make sure that you cover all the assessment objectives.

Contents of the study

Most of the examination syllabuses will expect your study notebook or folio to include the following.
- An introduction to the child(ren) you are studying. Give details of age, physical characteristics, personality, family background and environment.
- The area(s) of development you have selected to study and the reasons for your choice.
- Your observations over a period of time, perhaps as a diary, relating these observations to your selected area of development.
- A comparison of the development of the child(ren) you are studying with the relevant norms in textbooks, and with other children.
- An evaluation of your work. Did it follow your original plan, and how could it be improved?
- Your conclusions, which can include comments upon the value to you of the piece of work you have done and any follow-up work it could lead to.

The observational study

Do	Don't
* write legibly — if your handwriting is poor, would someone type it for you, or could you use a word processor?	* include class notes in your study
* read your work through. Re-write parts which don't make sense or are too wordy	* include details of the mother's pregnancy unless this relates to the child's physical or mental development (e.g. handicapped because of mother's rubella during pregnancy)
* design effective ways of dividing your work up and produce an interesting cover	* include items of value, e.g. birth certificate, or items of sentimental value, e.g. child's drawings. They can be copied, photographed or photocopied
* use clear headings and dates. You may be able to colour code to show that you have included all aspects	* glue in photographs; use photographic corners, then they can be removed if the study has to be sent away
* discuss your work with your teacher as you go along. Accept his/her advice and criticism	* include long passages or photocopied pages from textbooks (your teacher or the examiner will not read them). You should make your own interpretation in your own words
* include relevant quotations from books but indicate that they are not your own original work	* leave everything until the last minute
* include a clear contents list or index page and a bibliography	
* present neatly cut and mounted illustrations on plain paper, well labelled	
* keep a record of the number of words you have written	

Final points

☐ Keep your work safe. If it is lost you will have to start all over again.

☐ Check the arrangements for the return of your study. Your school may have to keep it for assessment purposes until after you have left school.

☐ If the child you are studying suddenly becomes unavailable, because the family leaves the district, or the child is seriously ill, for example, you may have to continue your work using another child; check with your syllabus notes of guidance. In special circumstances the Examining Group will consider a letter of appeal from your school.

☐ If you do not achieve the grade you are aiming for and wish to re-sit, your coursework can often be added to or altered and submitted for reassessment.

☐ Make sure you hand in your work, in good time, complete with your name and candidate's number and the name of your school or college.

Work Unit 1 - Preliminary observational exercises

Work Unit 1 - Preliminary observational exercises

Below are five tasks. They are designed to prepare you for your own child study. They are arranged in order, so that each task requires more decision-making about:
- how you should obtain the information you need
- how you should organize the study
- how you should present and evaluate the information you obtain.

Physical milestones

Task 1
Collect together some books or leaflets which give you general guidance about a child's physical development.

Task 2
Look closely at the pictures and then complete the following exercise.

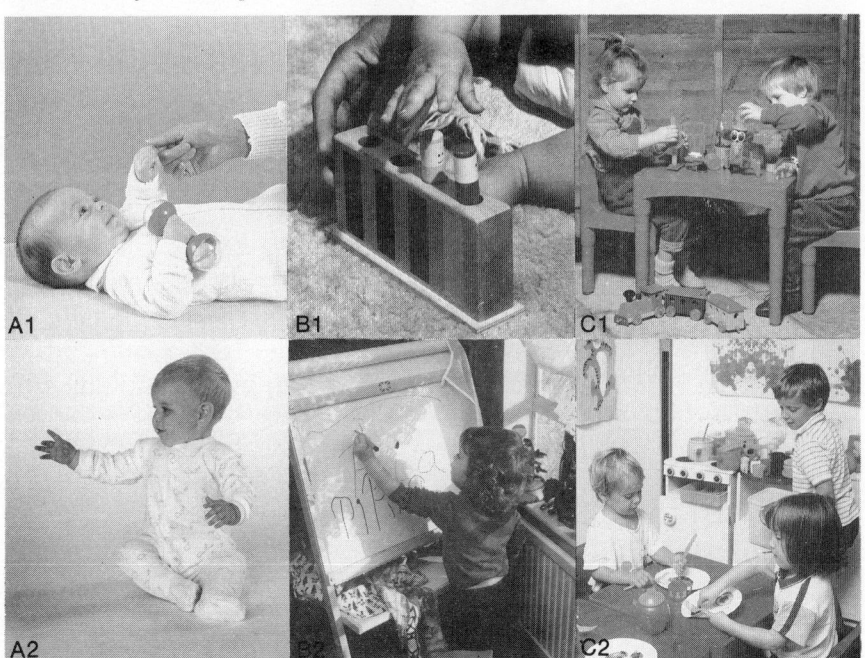

a) i. At what age and stage of development are the children in photos A1 and A2?
   ii. What details of the face and hands would make you believe that baby A1 is younger than baby A2?
   iii. What details of muscular co-ordination are present in baby A2 which are not present in A1?
   iv. Are there any other reasons why you have given the ages and stages in your answer to question i?
b) i. Look at the way each child in B1 and B2 is gripping the object. Which is the most mature grasp? What is the technical name for each grasp shown?

ii. What age and stage of manipulative co-ordination has each child reached? Give reasons for your answers.

iii. Why can you only give a general idea of the ages of these two stages of development?

c) i. Look at the children in C1 and C2 closely. What activities are they involved in? What are their approximate ages? How advanced are their manipulative skills?

ii. How would you describe the expressions on the faces of the children? Are they enjoying themselves?

iii. How are the activities they are involved in helping their muscular co-ordination and hand/eye co-ordination?

Collect together some pictures or photographs of older children (four, five and six year-olds). Study the pictures and write about the ages and stages of physical development you think they have reached.

Task 3

Watch some videos which show children of various ages involved in random activities, in groups or alone, with or without adults. Suitable films include:

Baby and Co. 2	Yorkshire Television
The Child's World	ILEA Learning Research Branch
The First Ten Months	Oxford Educational Resources Ltd.
Family Matters (Parts 5 & 6)	Concord Films Council Ltd.
The First Years of Life	LMSO, The Open University

Before you watch the film, decide what you want to find out. You could be looking at how children use their hands, or ways in which children achieve balance, or crawling and walking skills. It is easier to concentrate on one aspect to start with. How will you record your observations? You could:

☐ prepare a check list beforehand and mark off each achievement as you see it

☐ jot down notes or make sketches as you watch and copy them up later

☐ prepare a chart of the 'accepted norms' (capabilities of the average child) of a particular aspect and see how it compares with the child(ren) in the video

☐ talk into a tape recorder, recording the interesting aspects which you see.

After watching the film(s) write down your report, concentrating on the aspects you decided upon.

Task 4

In order to observe a single child, try to arrange to visit one of the following:

☐ a play group or nursery class
☐ a childminder and children

- a play park or recreation ground
- the home of the child you are going to study for your exam.

If you are nervous about visiting to observe you may be able to 'role play' the situation in school before you go. Within your group, select people to play the child, the parent or playgroup leader and the student who is observing. Rehearse what might take place at the first meeting.

Before you go:
- decide which aspect of physical development you will concentrate upon
- decide how long you will spend with the child(ren) — up to 30 minutes is long enough to start with
- decide how you will record your observations (as in Task 3)
- research the 'accepted norms' of children in the same age group as the one(s) you are studying
- research what can make a child slower or more advanced than other children in his age group, e.g. being overweight can affect progress
- collect together all the things you will need: clipboard, pencil, tape recorder, toy or activity for child, checklist of questions etc.

When you arrive:
- explain to the adult in charge what you wish to do, and obtain permission
- observe your 'target' child closely but try not to appear to be doing so
- play with the child, talk to him and gain his confidence: this will help you to observe him more easily
- fill in your checklist or make short notes as inconspicuously as possible.

Afterwards:
- copy your notes and make your report as soon after the observation period as possible whilst it is still fresh in your mind.

Task 5
Assess the value of the tasks you have completed.
- was your preliminary planning thorough?
- did your plans work?
- did you finish all the tasks? If not, why not?
- could your plans have been better? What went wrong?
- do you need more practice with observation skills?
- have these tasks given you the confidence to start your child study, folio or diary?

Do you understand the relationship between observing specific areas of development in the child(ren) you are studying and relating these observations to the following:
- accepted norms in textbooks
- comparisons with other children
- comparisons with current trends?

Work Unit 2 – Observational study

Mobility

By mobility we mean the acquisition of sitting, crawling and walking skills.

The Brief
To observe a child (Claire) over a period of 6 months, recording her progress in the acquisition of mobility skills;
to compare this child with children in the same age group and with textbook 'accepted norms';
and to evaluate my work.

Task 1 Forward Planning
  a) Inform Claire's parents of my plans and ask permission to study their child. The following is my letter.

  Dear Jane and Tom,
  　　　　　As part of my GCSE Child Development course I must observe and compile a study of a child. I would be most grateful if you will allow me to study Claire for a period of about six months, visiting her approximately once a week. All the work I do will be confidential and you of course can read it. Please sign the slip below if you agree to this arrangement.

  　　　　　　　　　Yours sincerely, ...

  Confirmation
  Signature of parent(s) . . . .
  　　　　　　　Date . . . .

  b) Make a rough plan of:

   * when my visits will take place   * how I will record my visits
   * how I will organize my work   * how I will file and keep my work
  c) Make a checklist of all the aspects which will need to be covered in my study and tick these off as they are completed.
  d) Research the background information on physical development, especially mobility skills. Suitable books are:

   From Birth to Five Years, Mary Sheridan (NFER/Nelson)
   Baby and Child, Penelope Leach (Penguin)
   Reader's Digest Mothercare Book 0–10 Years (Reader's Digest)
   A Practical Guide to Child Development (Bk 1), Valda Reynolds (Stanley Thornes)
   Living with Babies and Toddlers, (Open University Press)

e) Start a collection of resources such as booklets, leaflets, photographs, charts, drawings, magazine articles and audio tapes which may help to illustrate my study.
f) Plan and draw out suitable charts, record sheets, questionnaires and checklists for recording my observations when visiting Claire.

Task 2   First home visit

The main aims of this visit are:
- to make contact with the child, play with her and make general observations
- to chat with Jane (the mother) about my study and collect background information, e.g. Claire's name, age, date of birth, weight, height and physical characteristics (use photo here)
- the family: nuclear or extended, number in family, siblings and relations, mother/father, type of jobs, interests, relationship; any details which may influence the development of their child; draw a family tree
- the home: describe the building and its amenities, draw a plan of the house; does Claire have her own bedroom or does she share, where does Claire play? Is there a garden?
- the environment: is it a caring, healthy environment? Do Claire's parents provide stimulating surroundings and activities? Draw a map of where the house is situated and mark the location of shops, parks, schools, playgroups, health centre, etc.

I will write up my report as soon as possible whilst the details are still fresh in my mind. I must remember to date all my reports. I will use photographs or drawings of Claire, her parents, relations, home etc. if possible and I must label these.

Task 3   Second home visit

The aims of this visit are:
- to obtain more background information
- to begin to observe Claire in familiar home situations, for example:

  * playing with her brother   * having a bath   * eating lunch
  * greeting daddy   * getting ready for bed   * playing in the garden

My checklist points will be:
- Claire's personality: is she quiet, reserved, energetic, curious or friendly?
- Claire's behaviour: how does she respond to 'No!'? Have her parents started to discipline her yet? What happens when she is tired, excited, hungry or uncomfortable?
- Claire's reactions: to her parents, to her brother, her grandparents, other relations. Has she any favourite toys, food or clothing?

The observational study

Task 4 Third home visit

The aim of this visit is to find out what Claire can do. On this visit I will as far as possible fill in a record sheet (like the ones below and on the next two pages) showing the stages Claire has reached in her physical development. I will then be able to compare this with the progress Claire makes over the next six months. At this stage I will also note on the chart the 'accepted norms' for this age for comparison.

Comparative Record Sheet 1

Child's Forename .... Age 6 months Place ....

Date	Observations √ or X
When lying down raises head strongly	
Sits up easily for a few moments without support	
When hands are held can pull herself up	
Kicks legs freely and vigorously	
Turns head from side to side when sitting	
Rolls over on to stomach pushes down with feet when held in standing position	
When lying on abdomen pushes up strongly, lifting head and chest	
Crawling movements begin	
Uses whole hand to grasp objects	
Passes a toy from one hand to the other	
Other Observations	

Accepted norms at six months

By six months he can lift his entire head, chest and upper abdomen

Lying down, raises head, puts feet in mouth

Hands held – pulls herself up

Straight back when held in a sitting position

Pushes down with feet when held in standing position

© Valda Reynolds and Stanley Thornes (Publishers) Ltd 1990, *Coursework Explained: Child Development*

Work Unit 2 - Observational study

 Task 5
On further home visits I will observe Claire's progress and keep detailed results in the form of a diary. I will relate my observations to my chosen study area. A computer would be useful so that I could constantly update my observations.

Comparative Record Sheet 2

Child's Forename   Age 9 months   Place

Accepted norms at nine months

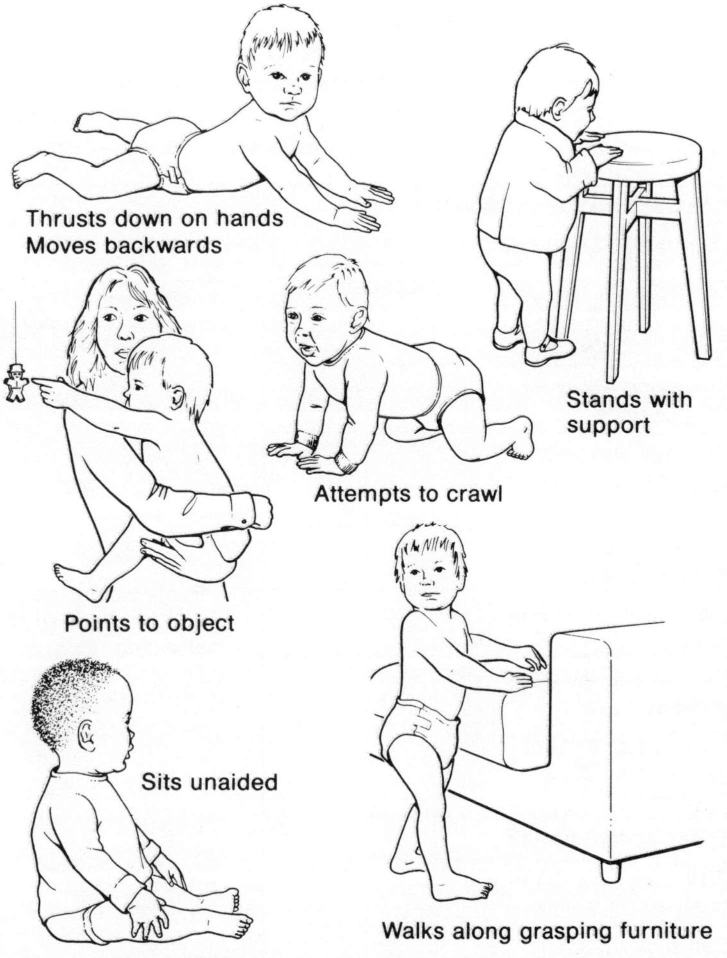

Date 3 months later	Observations ✓ or X
Can pull up to sitting position	
Can sit unaided for several minutes	
Is attempting to crawl	
Makes progress by rolling or shuffling	
Can pull herself up by the furniture	
Can stand — supported — for a few moments	
Can walk along by grasping furniture	
Uses finger and thumb for grasping	
Points and pokes objects	
Manipulates toys	
Other Observations	

Thrusts down on hands
Moves backwards

Stands with support

Points to object

Attempts to crawl

Sits unaided

Walks along grasping furniture

© Valda Reynolds and Stanley Thornes (Publishers) Ltd 1990, *Coursework Explained: Child Development*

Evaluation
After three months' observation I can judge the amount of progress which Claire has made.
☐ Has she made slow, rapid, or average progress?
☐ How does she compare with the accepted norms?
☐ What social, physical and environmental factors have influenced her progress?

- ☐ Has she had any illnesses to slow down her progress?
- ☐ Has she been encouraged or discouraged by her brother?
- ☐ What toys does she have which will help her to achieve crawling and walking skills? Can I suggest any others?

Task 6

For my final record sheet I want to compare Claire's progress with that of a child of similar age. Claire's mother has a friend with a boy (Robert) aged one year, who is willing to let me observe the two children together. I will be able to:

- ☐ compare Claire's progress with the accepted norms
- ☐ compare her progress with a child of the same age
- ☐ compare the difference between the progress of a girl and a boy and also other circumstances which may have influenced her progress.

Comparative Record Sheet 3

Children's Forenames   Place

Accepted norms at twelve months

	Observations	
	√ or X	√ or X
Date 3 months later		
Sits alone easily for long periods		
Can pull her/himself up easily but still prefers to crawl		
Is walking easily around furniture		
Walks with one hand held		
Can take a few steps unaided		
Lowers her/himself gently to a sitting position		
Tries to crawl upstairs		
Walks with the aid of a push-along trolley		
Can pick up small objects easily		
Uses hands to throw things		
Helping to dress and feed her/himself		
Other Observations		

Rests weight on feet and hands ready for standing

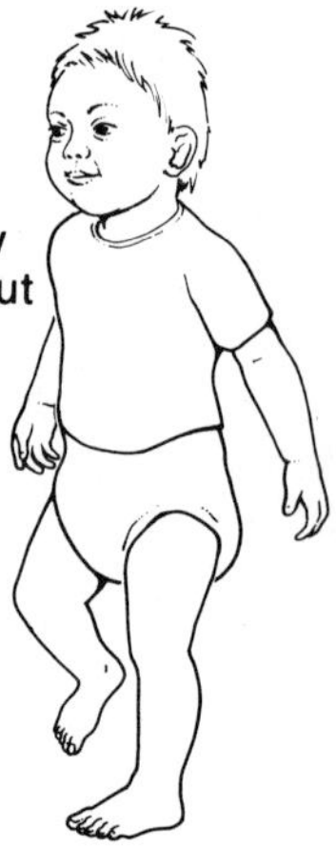

Takes a few steps without help

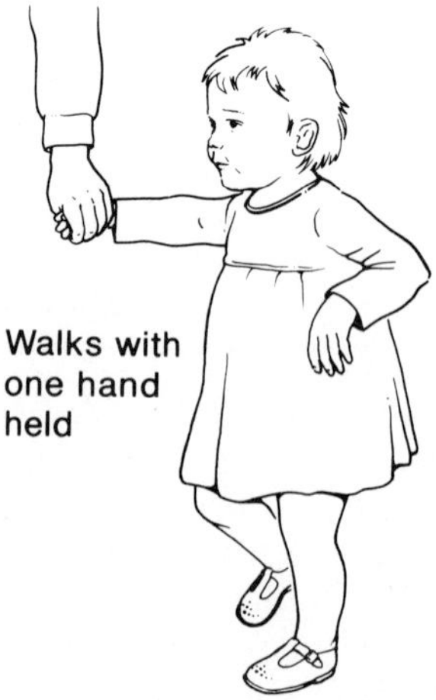

Walks with one hand held

Sits easily – turns from right to left

© Valda Reynolds and Stanley Thornes (Publishers) Ltd 1990, *Coursework Explained: Child Development*

Work Unit 2 - Observational study

 Task 7
This task consists of completing a self evaluation report.

Self Evaluation Report	Name
Developmental Study	Date started . . . . completed . . . .
Placement	(Home or playgroup?)
Time	(Length of time covered)
Visits	(Number of visits made)
Aims	Did I cover the aims as set out in my brief? (If any were not covered, give reasons)

Planning	My planning throughout was:
	   Very good ☐ good ☐ poor ☐
	Could the planning have been improved upon?
	   Yes ☐ No ☐
	What improvements could I have made?

Observations	Was I able to observe the child(ren) adequately and thoroughly? Yes ☐ No ☐ If not, why not?
Learning	What have I learned and what have I gained from my work? What have the child(ren) and the parents gained?

Enjoyment	I have enjoyed the work
	   A lot ☐ quite a lot ☐ not at all ☐
	Did I choose an interesting development area?
	   Yes ☐ No ☐
	How could I have made the work more interesting and enjoyable?

Improvements	Which parts were successful and which were not so successful? What improvements could I now suggest for improving the planning and recording of my work?
Skills	What skills have I used in this work? Are there some skills of which I should be making more use?
Assessment Objectives	Have I covered all the Assessment Objectives with the correct weightings? (See explanation in Examination Terms)
Continuation	Could the study of this area of development be continued further? Could I make some supporting material e.g. a toy, or information booklet, connected with my work? How does this detailed study fit into my other work in the subject? Has this work influenced my choice in deciding whether to continue with the study of Child Development even further?
Teacher's Comments	Date:

© Valda Reynolds and Stanley Thornes (Publishers) Ltd 1990, *Coursework Explained: Child Development*

Evaluation
I will ask the same questions as I did last time, and in addition:
- How did Claire compare with Robert?
- What reasons can I suggest for Claire making slower/quicker progress?
- Do some girls tend to develop some skills more quickly than boys and the other way about? Why?
- Which factors are most important in developing physical skills e.g. family, environment, health, sex of child, heredity etc?
- What positive steps can parents and carers take to encourage children to make satisfactory progress?

Work Unit 3 – Group observational study

Socialisation skills
and play

The Brief
To observe a group of children over a period of six weeks;
to choose one child to study in depth, and to record my observations of this child, comparing his level of social skills with his companions and text book norms;
to observe how he fits into the playgroup regime and analyse how the facilities offered by the playgroup influence the child's social development; and
to evaluate my work.

Task 1   Forward Planning
a) Check the arrangements made for my visit to the playgroup. When I attend playgroup 1 will:
- know the dates and times of my arrival
- always be punctual, arrive early to help with the setting out of equipment
- wear school uniform, but take protective clothing
- take a notepad and pencil and anything else needed to record my observations
- always be helpful and be prepared to clear up, take children to the toilet etc.
- remember that the most important thing is the safety of the children
- not sit chatting to friends, and remember that I am there to observe and to work
- write up my observations immediately after each visit
- have questions planned before I go, and discuss my work with the playgroup leader when convenient to her
- let the playgroup leader and my teacher know immediately if I am unable to attend
- have my attendance register signed each week and thank the organiser before I leave.

b) I will collect some information about the playgroup, before I go if possible, or during my first visit.

General
Name of the playgroup
Number and times of the sessions per week
Telephone number
Name of playgroup leader
Number of other helpers
Number of children attending   Age range
Price charged
Are handicapped children included?
Which areas do the children come from?
How much parental involvement is there?
What work will I be involved in?

Description

Detailed labelled plan of the room to include:

* activity areas   * reading area   * toy storage   * kitchen facilities   * heating arrangements   * placing of furniture   * cloakroom and toilets

Is there an outside area for play? Give a description.

Routine

Detailed timetable of playgroup session.
Why is the session so organised?
Do quiet periods follow activity sessions?

Aims

What are the aims of the playgroup and how do the staff try to fulfill these aims?
How are the children encouraged to socialise and develop their social skills,
□ by the staff?
□ by the toys and activities used?

c) I will consider:
□ what to look for on each visit to the playgroup e.g. the playgroup routine and its contribution to socialisation; the group of children who attend; the child I choose to study
□ how to select a particular child for my in-depth study and the reasons for studying him.

Some children particularly benefit from attending playgroups. Complete the chart.

Category	Reasons for benefit
Single or lonely children	
Those from ethnic minority groups	
Slow developers, timid, shy or handicapped children	
Those from violent or deprived homes	
Children living in high rise flats	
(Other categories)	

I will also consider:
□ how to obtain and record the child's background details
□ how to draw up charts comparing the child, his peers and children of the next stage of development
□ any difference between the child's development and the expected norms for his/her age.

Work Unit 3 – Group observational study

d) I will research the background information, remembering that social development is closely linked to all the other areas of development.

Suitable resources include:

Introduction to Child Development, Patricia Hicks (Longman)
The Human Body, (Galley Press)
Finding Out About Child Development, Valda Reynolds (Stanley Thornes)
People Making People, Ruth Bennet (Hutchinson)
Good Toy Guide, (A C Black/Play Matters)

Videos:
Child Behaviour — You, Guild Sound and Vision Ltd
Social Growth in Infants, University of Newcastle upon Tyne.

e) I will plan and produce observation sheets, charts, checklists and questionnaires to take on my playgroup visits.

These three-year-olds are only just beginning to enjoy group play. Two to three-year-olds have not learned to play together and prefer to play alongside each other. They are not ready for playgroup at that stage

Task 2 First Playgroup Visit

The main aims for my visit will be:

a) to collect general information about the playgroup as detailed on pages 15 and 16.
b) to observe a group of new entry children (aged 3–$3\frac{1}{2}$). What social skills do they have? (See the socialisation skills checklist.) Make a list of the social skills which a three-year-old requires when starting pre-school education.
c) to observe how the children are encouraged to socialise and the activities used to develop this. Is there a special area for developing socialisation skills?

d) I will try to interview the playgroup leader for general background information on the children, their social background, the local environment, community amenities, any social problems e.g. high unemployment, poor housing.
e) I will try to identify one child to study in greater detail. I will observe his stage of socialization and see what progress he makes over my period of study.

The third aim concerns the general observation of a target group of children to see how well they socialise and link this to the activities offered. Try to identify the children's socialisation skills. Observe their relationships with adults and with other children.

Observe how:
☐ the children behave when the parent leaves
☐ they react to the playgroup helpers
☐ the helpers treat the children
☐ the children mix together
☐ they play together and share activities
☐ the helpers deal with any solitary children — do they draw the children in?
☐ any aggressive, bullying children are dealt with.

Communication:
☐ what level of language have the children attained?
☐ do they chatter much to each other and to the helpers?
☐ do the helpers chatter much to them?
☐ how are communication skills developed? By joining in singing, nursery rhymes, games, reading sessions?
☐ is language essential for the development of socialisation?
☐ what about the child whose communication skills are very poor?

Independence:
☐ which children have a high level of independence?
☐ which social skills are important for making the children feel independent?
☐ do these skills give them confidence?
☐ how much teacher support do they require?
☐ do social skills encourage safety awareness?
☐ how safe is the playgroup generally and what contributions do the helpers make towards safety?

Roles and role-play:
☐ do the boys and girls mix together?
☐ do they play well together or do they argue?
☐ is gender stereotyping avoided and if so — how?
☐ are opportunities given for imitative play, role-play or modelling so that children have both male and female role models?
☐ are all types of discrimination (e.g. sexual, racial, cultural, religious) avoided?

Work Unit 3 - Group observational study

Socialisation skills checklist

Name _____   Date _____

Children aged 3 to 3½

Social Relationships	Name of child				
Co-operative with adults, eager to please					
Responds to kind discipline					
Reasonably self-confident					
Considers the need of others					
Willing to be parted from parent for a short time					
Shyness in strange circumstances					
Self-willed and aggressive					
Jealous of younger sibling					
Friendly with other children, wants to play with them					
Influenced by peer group					
Shares sweets and toys					
Enjoys social role-play e.g. mothers and fathers					
Social Skills (with minimal help)					
Dresses and undresses					
Can pull pants up and down					
Fastens simple shoe fastenings					
Can use spoon and fork at table					
Washes and dries hands					
Can use toilet					
Can pour water into a beaker from a jug					
Tries to tidy up toys					
Uses a handkerchief					
Says 'Please, 'Thank you', 'Excuse me'					

© Valda Reynolds and Stanley Thornes (Publishers) Ltd 1990, *Coursework Explained: Child Development*

The observational study

Behaviour:
- [ ] what are the major behavioural problems in the group, e.g. lying, bullying, aggression, stealing, biting, hitting etc? What are the underlying causes?
- [ ] how are such problems dealt with by the helpers?

What activities are offered to develop socialisation skills?

Social characteristics checklist

Children aged 3 to 4

	Name of child			
Cooperative with adults				
Reasonably independent				
Responds well to discipline				
Friendly with other children				
Has special friends				
Average language ability				
Approaches new tasks with confidence				
Concentrates on activity for average 5 mins 10 mins 15 mins				
Kind and caring attitude				
Willing to share toys, sweets				
Can control negative feelings e.g. anger, jealousy, fear, frustration, quite well				
Problem areas				
Play stage: solitary, parallel, group				

Analysis and Evaluation

© Valda Reynolds and Stanley Thornes (Publishers) Ltd 1990, *Coursework Explained: Child Development*

To help achieve the fourth aim, I must produce a questionnaire for the playgroup leader asking such questions as:
- do the children come from varied cultural backgrounds?
- are they mainly from rural or urban communities?
- how much parental support is involved?
- do you welcome children with physical handicaps or emotional disturbances?
- do you organise many outings?
- how much contact do you have with local schools and other sections of the community?

Lastly, to fulfil my fifth aim, I will identify one child to study in depth, if possible one whom I can obtain background information about, and who fits into a group who benefit most from attending playgroup.

I will try to obtain photographs of some of the children, the playgroup premises, some activities in progress, outdoor activities; examples of the children's work; a map showing the amenities, taped interviews with children, parents, playgroup staff.

Task 3   Second, third and fourth playgroup visits

The main aims for my visits will be:

a) to observe the target group closely in these circumstances:

* when they arrive   * when parents depart   * in the cloakroom   * eating and drinking   * at solitary play   * at group play   * with adults   * when collected   * when frustrated, unhappy, distressed, nervous, intimidated, happy, excited

b) To observe Nathan (my special study) to see:
- how socially developed he is
- how well he fits in with his peers
- how he reacts to adults
- if he has any behavioural problems
- if I can research his family background
- if I can make a comparative study of Nathan and his peers.

c) To record the results of my observations using a variety of techniques.

Nathan is nearly five and will go to primary school in September. He is one of a few black children attending the group and comes from a large family. The children in the family are generally happy, sociable and well-mannered. The family have a low income and can afford few toys or outings.

The observational study

Skills		Name of child		
Relationships Age				
Wishes to please adults				
Developing sense of humour				
Good control of emotions				
Argues with other children				
Enjoys competitive complex games				
Sympathetic to those in distress				
Rather careless and untidy				
Answers back and contradicts				
Increasingly independent				
Prefers to play in groups of own sex				
Is a leader				

	Uses knife, fork and spoon	Fastens shoelaces	Uses and flushes toilet	Hangs up clothing	Knows right foot from left	Brushes teeth
Name Age						
Name Age						
Name Age						

Analysis and Evaluation

© Valda Reynolds and Stanley Thornes (Publishers) Ltd 1990, *Coursework Explained: Child Development*

Work Unit 3 - Group observational study

Social development checklist

Observations over a 6-week period Age	Name of child					
Integrating with other children						
Accepts separation from parents						
Responds well to adult helpers						
Is less/more shy, frightened, timid						
Is less/more aggressive, attention seeking						
Longer span of attention						
Able to control emotions better						
Is more cooperative						
Shares and takes turns more readily						
Fewer/more nervous habits e.g. nail biting						
Progress with language development						
Has made progress with social skills e.g. use of toilet, washing, dressing, eating						
Stage of play: solitary, parallel, group						
Analysis of each child over the six week period						

© Valda Reynolds and Stanley Thornes (Publishers) Ltd 1990, *Coursework Explained: Child Development*

Task 4   Fifth and sixth playgroup visits
The main aims of these visits will be:
    a) to continue my observations and evaluations of the group and in-depth observation of Nathan,

b) to note any changes and developments in social awareness of the children, and if possible,
c) to become involved in a group activity, possibly at a later date, e.g.:

* a playgroup picnic   * outing to a pleasure park   * visit to a pantomime   * birthday party   * fund raising event

As this is a short period of time I will not expect to find major changes as noted in my second aim. I hope to be able to visit the playgroup for a single follow-up visit in three to six months' time to make some longer-term observations.

Task 5
Take part in a practical activity connected with my child study.

In this case, the activity is a playgroup outing to the local pleasure park. I will use this experience to observe how:
☐ children react to a new experience
☐ they relate to known and unknown adults
☐ they socialise and play together
☐ they behave when tired, frustrated, excited etc.
☐ ready they are to share and take turns
☐ independent they are when using social skills such as dressing, eating, use of toilet etc.

I will especially observe the behaviour of my target group and Nathan.

Forward planning
☐ Find out and note the practical details e.g.:

* which park?   * time of departure and return   * transport arrangements   * number of children going   * number of adults going   * planned activities   * packed meals to be taken?   * money needed

☐ How can I help? Volunteer to take responsibility for one child, look after clothing, plan an activity such as a race, or make and distribute a plan of the park.
☐ How will I record my observations? With charts, questionnaires, or photographs?
☐ How will I record the activities during the day? I would like to ask the children to draw pictures in the park and them make these into a book called 'Our Day Out'. I must therefore take crayons and paper with me.
☐ List the things I must take, e.g. clipboard, pencil, notepad, camera, observation charts, questionnaires, raincoat, towel, plastic bags, food, money, drawing pad and crayons.

The value of the activity is that it is an exciting experience for the children, with opportunities for social contact between parents, children and playgroup helpers. It reinforces positive attitudes within the playgroup and contributes to the general education of the children.

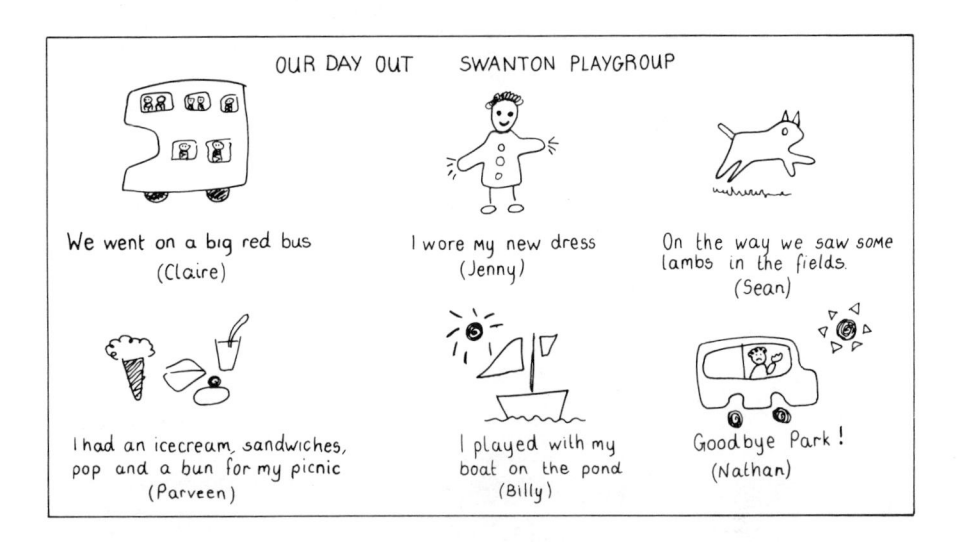

OUR DAY OUT   SWANTON PLAYGROUP

We went on a big red bus (Claire)

I wore my new dress (Jenny)

On the way we saw some lambs in the fields. (Sean)

I had an icecream, sandwiches, pop and a bun for my picnic (Parveen)

I played with my boat on the pond (Billy)

Goodbye Park! (Nathan)

Our day out

I will mount all the children's drawings on card and put them into a book.

Evaluation
Did the planning work? List the things that went wrong and those which were especially good. Did the adults enjoy the outing? Were they tired, happy or pleased?

How did the children benefit from the experience?
☐ did they mix well?
☐ did they enjoy the trip?
☐ did they become over-excited?
☐ were there any quarrels?
☐ were they suitably dressed?
☐ did they enjoy their food?
☐ did they enjoy the planned activities?
☐ were they very tired?

What are the general impressions of the day?

* very successful   * well planned   * we attempted too much
* the park was not really suitable   * everyone enjoyed it   * everyone wants to go again

What improvements could be made for next time?

* take fewer children or more helpers   * go to a smaller park
* make a better time plan   * go to a park without water

Task 6 Follow-up activities

I will collect pictures of some of the group activities at the playgroup which encourage social integration and development. These activities could include: sand and water play, shop, musical toys, group collage etc.

I will make a compendium of toys and activities used in the playgroup which aid social development, showing those which are the most popular, how the children play with them and others which would be desirable.

Task 7 Self-evaluation report

Use the standard format self-evaluation report (page 13) with any additions or amendments considered necessary.

Work Unit 4 - Observational study

Work Unit 4 - Observational study

Manipulative skills and creativity

To observe a child (Tom) over a period of six months;
to record his progress in the acquisition of manipulative skills;
to give opportunities for showing his creative skills;
to compare his abilities and rate of progress with other children in the same age group and with 'accepted' norms, and to evaluate my work.

This work unit example uses a male student.

Task 1 Forward planning

The planning of this work unit is the same as for Work Unit 2, on p. 8. These additional books may be useful under (d).

Child Development, (Diagram Group)
The Baby Care Book, Dr M. Stoppard (Dorling Kindersley)
Rooms to Grow Up In, Rosie Fisher (New Burlington Books)

Checklist for manipulative skills

Child's forename	Age 5 years
Date	Observations ✓ or X
Cuts out shapes	
Completes a jigsaw of 25 pieces	
Picks up small beads	
Threads large beads on wool	
Build 3 steps from 6 bricks	
Holds pencil correctly	
Traces a picture	
Turns the pages of a book	
Ties shoelaces	
Dresses and undresses a doll	
Can use some household tools (supervised)	

Place Home

Accepted norms

Completes a jigsaw of 26 pieces

Turns the pages of a book

Builds 3 or 4 steps from model

Holds a pencil correctly

Manipulative skills

© Valda Reynolds and Stanley Thornes (Publishers) Ltd 1990, *Coursework Explained: Child Development*

Tasks 2 and 3 First and second home visits

The purpose of these visits is to obtain background information and to observe Tom in his home.

Tom lives with one parent. His mother and father split up two years ago and he is now aged five, and living with his mother in a council flat. Tom's mother, Margaret, welcomes my project. She likes Tom having an older boy to relate to and to look after him occasionally

Task 4 Third home visit

I will use this visit to compare Tom's standard of manipulative skills with my checklist (p. 27) of the accepted norms.

Checklist for creative ability

Activity	✓ or X	Enjoyment * * * * * *	Accepted norms
Writes a few letters			

Copies a square
     a cross
     a triangle			

Draws a recognisable human shape			
Draws a house with door, windows, chimney			
Colours a picture — staying within the outline			
Names three primary colours			
Embroiders, using large stitches			
Models with clay or playdough			
Makes models from card, paper, wood			
Makes collage pictures from paper, string, buttons etc.			
Uses large cartons to make ships, trains etc.			

Writes a few letters

Copies a square, cross and triangle

Embroiders using large stitches

Draws a house

Draws a recognisable human shape

Creative ability

© Valda Reynolds and Stanley Thornes (Publishers) Ltd 1990, *Coursework Explained: Child Development*

Work Unit 4 - Observational study

Task 5 Fourth home visit

I will check Tom's creative skills and observe which activities give him the most pleasure. I can then plan a list of creative activities to do with Tom, requiring varying levels of skill.

Task 6

Plan a series of creative activities for Tom of ascending levels of skill, requiring little or no help from me. Here are some suggestions:

1. a 'junk' toy made from empty small cartons, cardboard cylinders, tissue paper, buttons, string etc.
2. a windmill for outdoors using thin card
3. a bead necklace using playdough or magazine paper
4. a jigsaw using a picture he likes
5. a wooden hoopla game with rings made from card

Pictures of these with brief instructions for making them are shown below.

1. **Totem pole**
Cover a cardboard cylinder with coloured paper or poster paint.

Use egg boxes for eyes and nose, cut ears and top piece from coloured card.

Paint decorations on, add tissue paper frills, mount on paper tray.

2. **Windmill**
Cut from each corner towards centre. Push a pin through the four holes shown and draw corners to the centre. Push pin or tack through centre X to form a pinwheel. Place a small bead on the tack and knock the tack into a piece of cane.

3. **Necklace**
Make bead from play-dough, push knitting needle through to make hole. Paint on pattern. Thread beads on cord.

OR

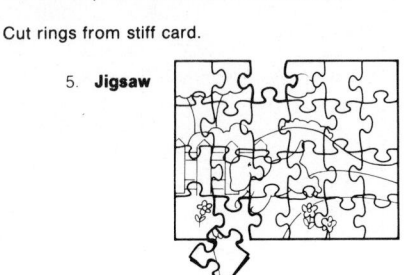

Cut shape from coloured magazine page, paste one side and wind round needle to form bead.

4. **Hoop-la game**
Cut out shape of tortoise, pig, elephant, etc. from thin plywood. Paint on large and small spots. Screw a hook into each spot. Paint numbers underneath.

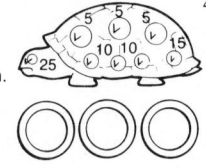

Cut rings from stiff card.

5. **Jigsaw**

Creative activities

The aims of these activities are:
a) to encourage Tom to use and develop his creative skills;
b) to give him opportunities for satisfaction and success by grading the activities carefully, giving praise and encouragement and only helping when necessary;

c) to encourage safety at all times and make each project an opportunity to emphasise good safety procedures with tools and materials;
d) to encourage a reasonable amount of tidiness, protecting surfaces and oneself and cleaning up afterwards;
e) to help Tom to persevere, cope with frustration and failure and try again if things go wrong, and
f) to offer a choice of materials to include wood, textiles, glues, card, clay, paint and crayons and supervised use of tools such as scissors, hammer, drill, fretsaw and brushes.

On each visit when I introduce a creative activity I will make a record of my observations using the question list below for guidance. I will try to take photographs of what Tom does.

	Date
What did we choose to make?	Why?
What materials did we choose?	Why?
What tools did we use?	
Safety points we observed.	
Were there any dangerous moments?	Why?
How were colour and pattern applied?	
How dextrous is Tom? Does he use tools well?	

How long was his average span of attention? How did I manage to retain his interest?

Who did most, Tom or myself?

Was Tom pleased with the finished object? Did he play with it?

Did Tom enjoy this project less/more than the other projects?

Task 7 Evaluation

Over the six months' observation period, how have Tom's manipulative and creative skills developed? Has he made good, average or slow progress?

Consult the checklists on page 27 and page 28. In what ways have these skills developed? Have I contributed to this progress?

What factors are important to the development of these skills, e.g. adult interest, encouragement, planning, stimulating environment, availability of materials and tools, sensible selection of projects?

Has Tom enjoyed the experiences I have provided and benefited from the company of an older boy?

How could the project be developed further?

Complete a *self evaluation report* as you did for previous work units with any necessary amendments or additions.

Observational study - further ideas

When you have studied the ideas presented in Work Units two, three, and four you can develop your own format and methods of working. Other specialist areas for in-depth study are suggested below.

Communication and language development

This may be undertaken with a fairly young baby over a period of nine to twelve months. The observations would start with the first method of communication, crying, through the stages of lip and tongue movements, cooing, chuckling, babbling, vowel sounds, understanding and repeating of first words, use of vowels and consonants and saying a few words with meaning. It could include comparisons between peers, textbook norms, language problems, and ideas on how to develop language skills. Alternatively, the study could involve a group of nursery school children: their comparative standards of language skills, the influence of their home environment, methods of stimulating communication and the progress noted over a series of visits.

Intellectual development and the influence of play

A study can be undertaken with a group of children at playgroup, or nursery school. Comparisons can be made between children of different age, sex, background, local environment and state of health; between siblings etc. Games, toys, literacy and numeracy aids and adult participation may all be studied as means of developing intellectual abilities amongst a target group. A similar study could be made of a child who is leaving the 'sensori-motor period' of babyhood, and entering the 'preconceptual period' of the toddler. This could show how personality and intelligence levels are developing, give indications of increasing intelligence, and include tests and observations which show the normal attainment standards. The choice of toys, games and activities to stimulate the child should be shown.

Other interesting areas upon which to base your ideas for investigative work include:
- the developing senses: sight, hearing, touch, taste, feel
- developing creativity through children's art, music and play
- the effect of the local environment on the child(ren) being studied
- socialisation and the effects of family and school
- acquisition of numeracy and the aids available
- the slow developer: the child with developmental problems.

COMPONENT TWO

Practical items

Guidelines

All Home Economics syllabuses must include a practical element for assessment. The Child Development syllabuses achieve this in part by requiring candidates to produce an item or activity connected with a child(ren). There are three methods used by the six examining bodies of introducing the item. These are:

a) a free choice: the item must respond to the declared need of the child(ren);
b) a choice from a restricted selection presented yearly by the examining group;
c) the item must be linked to the Child Study or the Investigational Study.

It is important that the notes of guidance for the practical item component, as given in the selected syllabus, are studied and followed.

All practical items must be accompanied by written support work. If an item is submitted without its written support work, it will only receive a small proportion of the available marks (see Marks Weightings).

The syllabus should give you information on the following:
- ideas of what to make or the list of briefs from which to make a choice
- the assessment objectives to be covered
- the factors to be covered in your written work
- the purpose of this piece of coursework
- methods of moderation (i.e. school-based marking or external moderation by the examining board)
- inclusion of common elements and common themes
- length of time to be allocated to this component
- use of skills
- the marking criteria. These are very important and it is essential to realise that the finished item may carry only a small proportion of marks.

Usually the important issues are:

- * analysing a need
- * choice
- * suitability
- * justification
- * use of techniques
- * effectiveness of planning
- * modifications
- * evaluations

Guidelines

Mark Allocation	Mark Allocation (Average Range)
Area 1 Analysing the need Choosing the item and the materials by applying relevant knowledge Justifying the methods and materials selected Outlining the final plan	25%–50%
Area 2 Carrying out the planned course of action Using a variety of techniques and skills Adapting the original plan when needed	16%–33%
Area 3 Assessing and evaluating the effectiveness of the planning and execution Observing the items in use Suggesting modifications to the original plan	20%–50%

Design and Technology flow chart

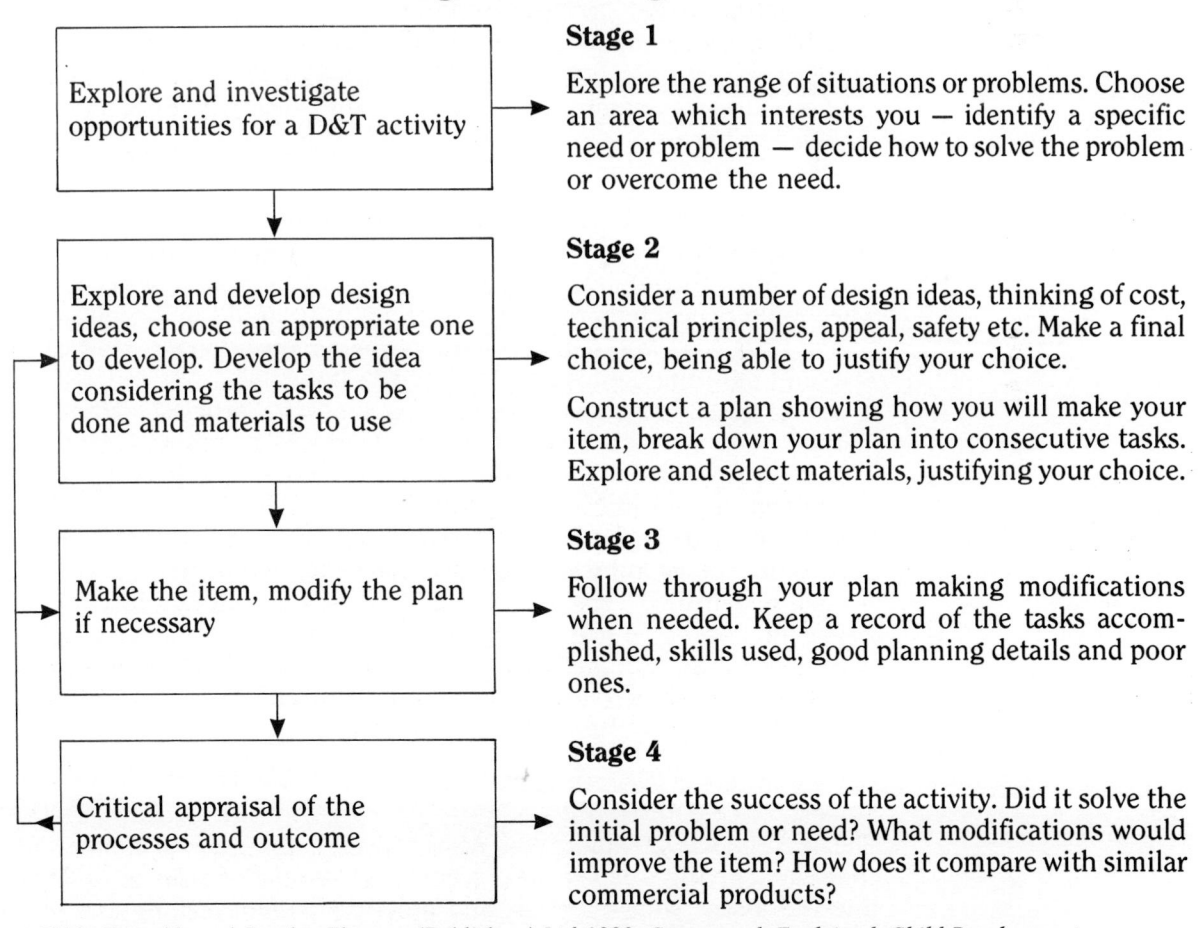

Explore and investigate opportunities for a D&T activity

Stage 1

Explore the range of situations or problems. Choose an area which interests you — identify a specific need or problem — decide how to solve the problem or overcome the need.

Explore and develop design ideas, choose an appropriate one to develop. Develop the idea considering the tasks to be done and materials to use

Stage 2

Consider a number of design ideas, thinking of cost, technical principles, appeal, safety etc. Make a final choice, being able to justify your choice.

Construct a plan showing how you will make your item, break down your plan into consecutive tasks. Explore and select materials, justifying your choice.

Make the item, modify the plan if necessary

Stage 3

Follow through your plan making modifications when needed. Keep a record of the tasks accomplished, skills used, good planning details and poor ones.

Critical appraisal of the processes and outcome

Stage 4

Consider the success of the activity. Did it solve the initial problem or need? What modifications would improve the item? How does it compare with similar commercial products?

© Valda Reynolds and Stanley Thornes (Publishers) Ltd 1990, *Coursework Explained: Child Development*

Planning your practical item

This component should be treated as a decision-making, problem-solving exercise. A Design and Technology approach should be taken. Technology is an important foundation subject.

> 'The capacity to investigate, design, make and appraise is as important as the acquisition of knowledge'.
>
> *National Curriculum Technology*

This statement makes it clear that the making of the item and the finished article are only part of the activity; of equal importance are the planning, justification and evaluation processes. The four-stage flow chart on page 33 shows how the component should be tackled.

Stage 1
At stage one you explore the possibilities, identify a need and provide a possible solution. Here are some ways to go about it:
- know your syllabus well. The item you choose to make must come within the syllabus content
- study the selection of briefs given by the examination board (if your board sets briefs)
- choose an area which interests you and which you know something about
- have a class 'brainstorming' session, pooling ideas with direction from your teacher
- keep a written record of your exploration and selection procedures.

When you have selected a possible area, identify a need or a problem. Look at the area you have chosen, e.g. protective clothing for children, then narrow down the range of choice, e.g. protective clothing at playgroup, when walking near busy roads, at mealtimes. You should do the following:
- try to put your working brief in the form of a question e.g. How can a child's clothing contribute to his road safety?
- collect together a pile of resources, e.g. magazine articles, craft books, child care magazines, ideas leaflets from manufacturers, clothing brochures, toy catalogues. Browse through them to help you link the problem in your brief to its solution
- if the item to be made must relate to your child (or group) study, consider the appropriate age and stage of development
- having identified a specific need and a possible solution, justify your selection and give reasons why you discarded some of your ideas
- consider a range of methods of recording your work, e.g. graphs, flow charts, design plans, drawings, photographs etc, and decide to use a good selection of these.

Stage 2
The next stage is to explore your design ideas, making a final appropriate choice and giving reasons. Make a consecutive plan of tasks to be done, test and assess your materials and processes before making any final decisions. Bear the following points in mind:

- make a list, and make sketches of a selection of possibilities as in the drawings

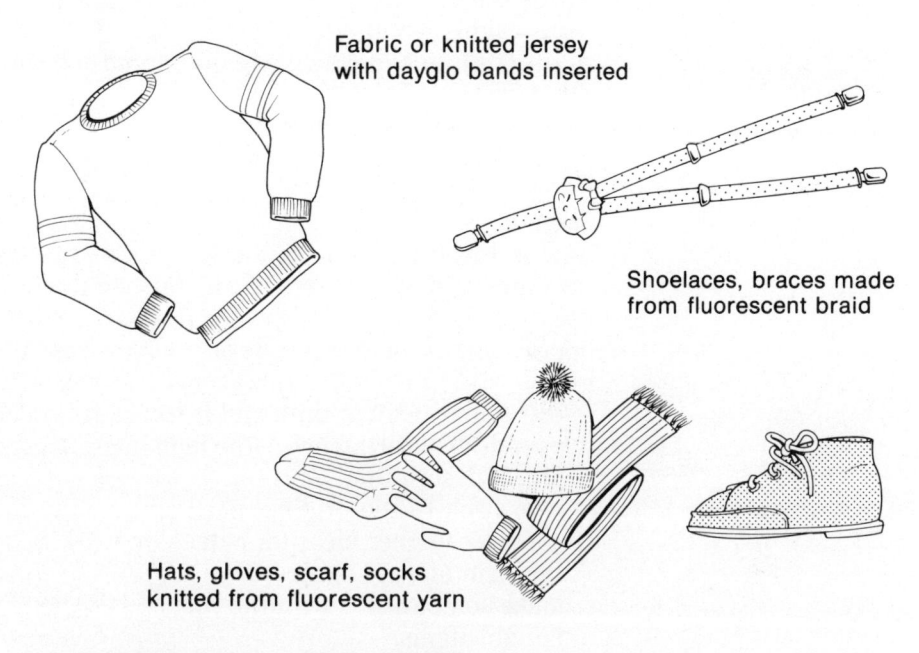

Fabric or knitted jersey with dayglo bands inserted

Shoelaces, braces made from fluorescent braid

Hats, gloves, scarf, socks knitted from fluorescent yarn

- consider your own levels of skill
- introduce some of the Common Elements (see Examination Terms), e.g. health, safety, efficiency, values, aesthetics, environment
- allow for restrictions such as shortage of time, money, technical equipment
- consider the storage of the item
- refer back to your brief, check that your choice fits its purpose and justifies your choice
- make a plan of action showing the sequence of your work
- gather together a selection of suitable materials e.g. yarns, fabrics, threads, wood, plastics, card, glues, paints, in differing colour combinations, strengths, thicknesses and textures
- relate the choice of materials to the requirements of the item e.g. strength, washability, softness, safety. Test and experiment with the materials before making a final selection
- make any modifications to your plan in response to your tests
- record your plan of action, experimental work, reasons for selection in several graphical ways.

Stage 3
Make the item, following through your plan of action. As you progress, use a varied selection of tools and equipment, modify and adapt your plan as you go along and keep a record of everything you do as you do it. Record each consecutive task; take photographs or make drawings. you should also record:
- the quantity and cost of materials used

- any details, small or large, of deviation from your original plan and why you made the changes
- how easy or difficult you found each task
- new skills which you learnt
- any faults and mistakes which occured and why and how they could be avoided.

Remember to keep your work safe and ready for assessment by your teacher.

Stage 4

Now is the time to make an analysis of the tasks performed and the strengths and weaknesses of the finished item. Refer back to Stage 1 — does your item solve the specific need or problem? Do you need to make improvements, modifications or comparisons? You should do the following:

- test out your item on a child; record its success or otherwise
- provide visual evidence of the item in use, e.g. photographs or drawings plus a description
- refer back to the original need and modify the item if necessary
- consider further ideas for extension work, relating it to the need and the item already made
- make comparisons with the cost and efficiency of other similar, shop-bought items
- complete the record of your work.

The design briefs which follow are not intended to be complete assignments. They are there for guidance and to stimulate your own ideas.

Design brief 1

The Brief
To design and make a toy for the child I am studying, which will encourage the area of development I have chosen to concentrate on. My specific area of development is physical coordination.

Stage 1
Exploration
The child in my study (Lesley) is four years old, very lively, with an enquiring mind and independent character. The problem is to make a toy for Lesley which:
- she can work for herself
- will make her wonder how it works
- will encourage her manipulative skills including fine motor skills and hand/eye coordination.

Solving the problem

I will carry out research using toy catalogues, magazines for parents, text-books dealing with development and books such as *The Good Toy Guide* (A & C Black).

I will observe children of this age at play at home, playgroup, in parks etc., and question parents and teachers about good popular designs which meet these criteria. I can look at toys in toy shops considering value for money, suitability of design, durability, attractiveness, safety, and hygiene. Lastly, I will sketch and make brief notes about the toys which fit the criteria.

Stage 2
Choice
Having taken Lesley into several toy shops and noticed that she seemed especially interested in wooden toys which moved and performed various activities I narrowed my choice down to those shown in the drawings.

I finally chose the spinning clown because:
- Nos. 2 and 3 would be too difficult for me to make
- No. 1 was not very interesting and could be difficult to work
- No. 5 would take a lot of time to make, including precision work, and lots of painting
- No. 4 would require Lesley to think about how to make it work, would hold her attention for some time and require precise movements to twist the rod and string

I would enjoy planning the toy and applying the technological and scientific principles
It will fit my original brief.

Practical items

1. Climbing Charlie
2. Pecking chickens
3. Egg laying hen
4. Spinning clown
5. Construction bricks

Designs of toys to choose from

Planning

This toy has a main shape with a rod through its centre. A string which is attached to both ends of the rod comes to a central point to make a hanging loop. When the rod is turned it twists the string around the ends of the rod. When the rod is released the string unwinds, the shape rotates and then rewinds, providing continuous movement for some minutes. The toy demonstrates several scientific principles which make it work. These include:
 a) energy is produced by a falling body
 b) a rotating body builds up an impetus.

The action depends upon gravity and rotation.

It is necessary to look for a basic shape which:

* will balance easily within its own area
* is big enough to contain its centre of gravity
* is interesting and satisfying

Design brief 1

I must be aware of cost, safety, strength, attractiveness, suitability for purpose, my level of skills and the availability of necessary tools.

My plan of action consists of ten tasks.

Task 1
First I must sketch several ideas for the basic shape of my toy and then select the most suitable using the criteria on page 38. I decided on design No. 1, because:
- design No. 1 can be painted to give a colourful, amusing finish
- this shape can be adapted to enclose its centre of gravity
- it is a pleasing shape which will amuse a child
- it is a simple shape which I will be able to cut out using a fretsaw
- the outline has no sharp edges and can be smoothed off for safety
- designs Nos. 2 and 4 are too complicated for me to cut out
- design No. 3 is not very interesting.

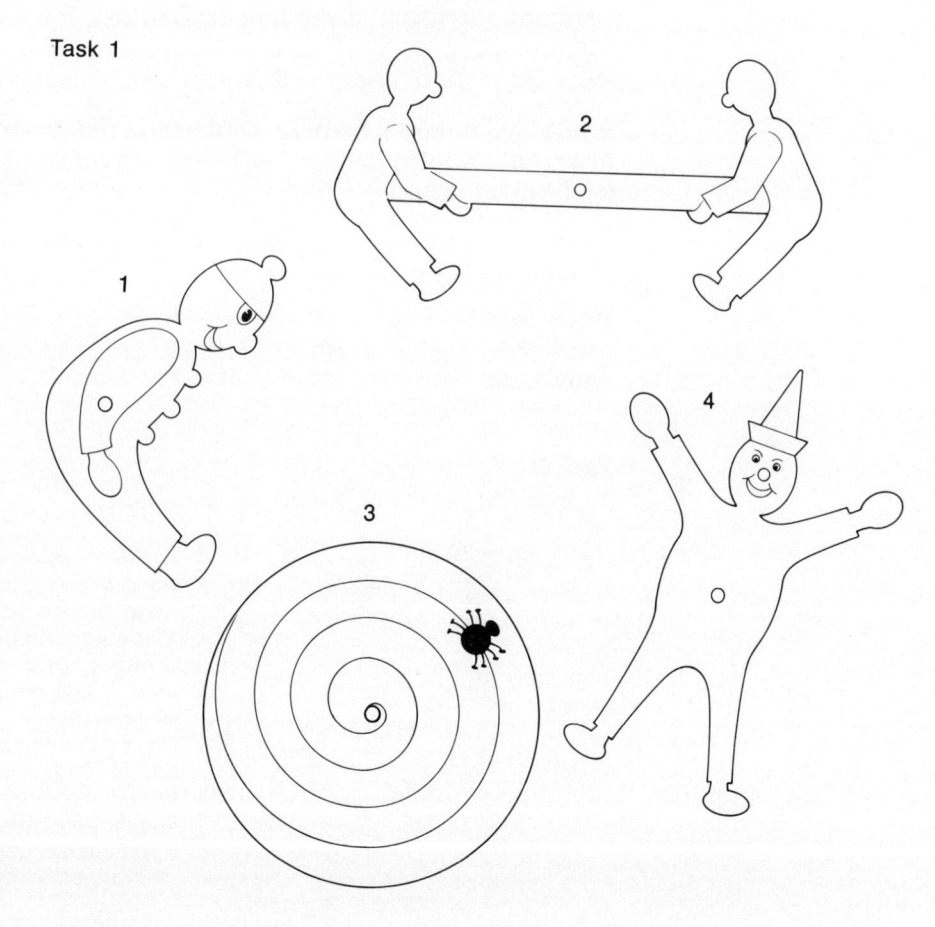

Task 1

Designs for a basic shape

Task 2
To consider and select the materials I shall use.

Toy part	Possible	Choice
Clown shape	wood — plywood, hardwood card — stiff or thin stiffened fabric hard plastic sheet perspex	plywood
The rod	dowelling a pencil rolled up card metal	dowelling
The cord	twine, string, nylon thread, wool, thin picture cord	fine string
Colour	lead-free oil paint, poster colour, felt tip pens, wood stain	lead-free oil paint

Reasons for Choices

Card and fabric are cheap and easy to cut, but too fragile. Plastic and perspex are a good choice, but expensive and not readily available. Plywood is quite cheap and sturdy, and it paints and cuts well.

A pencil is not long enough, card would not be strong enough. Metal is heavy and could be dangerous. Dowelling comes in different thicknesses, is cheap and can be drilled.

Nylon and wool thread can stretch. String is strong, cheap and comes in several thicknesses.

Water based colour quickly comes off, wood stain is expensive, lead-free paint gives a good finish. Often there are small amounts left over from household use.

Task 3
To find the centre of gravity of the shape.

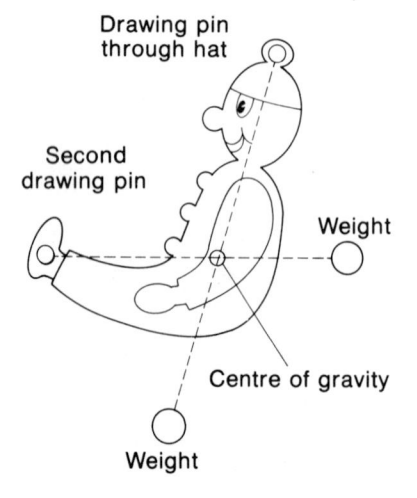

1. Draw shape onto stiff card. Cut it out.
2. Push drawing pin through centre of hat, hang loosely on a straight surface. Place weighted piece of string from drawing pin downwards.
3. Mark a line on the shape where the string falls.
4. Do the same, putting the drawing pin and string through the heel.
5. Where the string crosses the previous line is the centre of gravity.
6. If the central point is too near the edge, re-draw the shape to make it fatter.

Finding the centre of gravity

Design brief 1

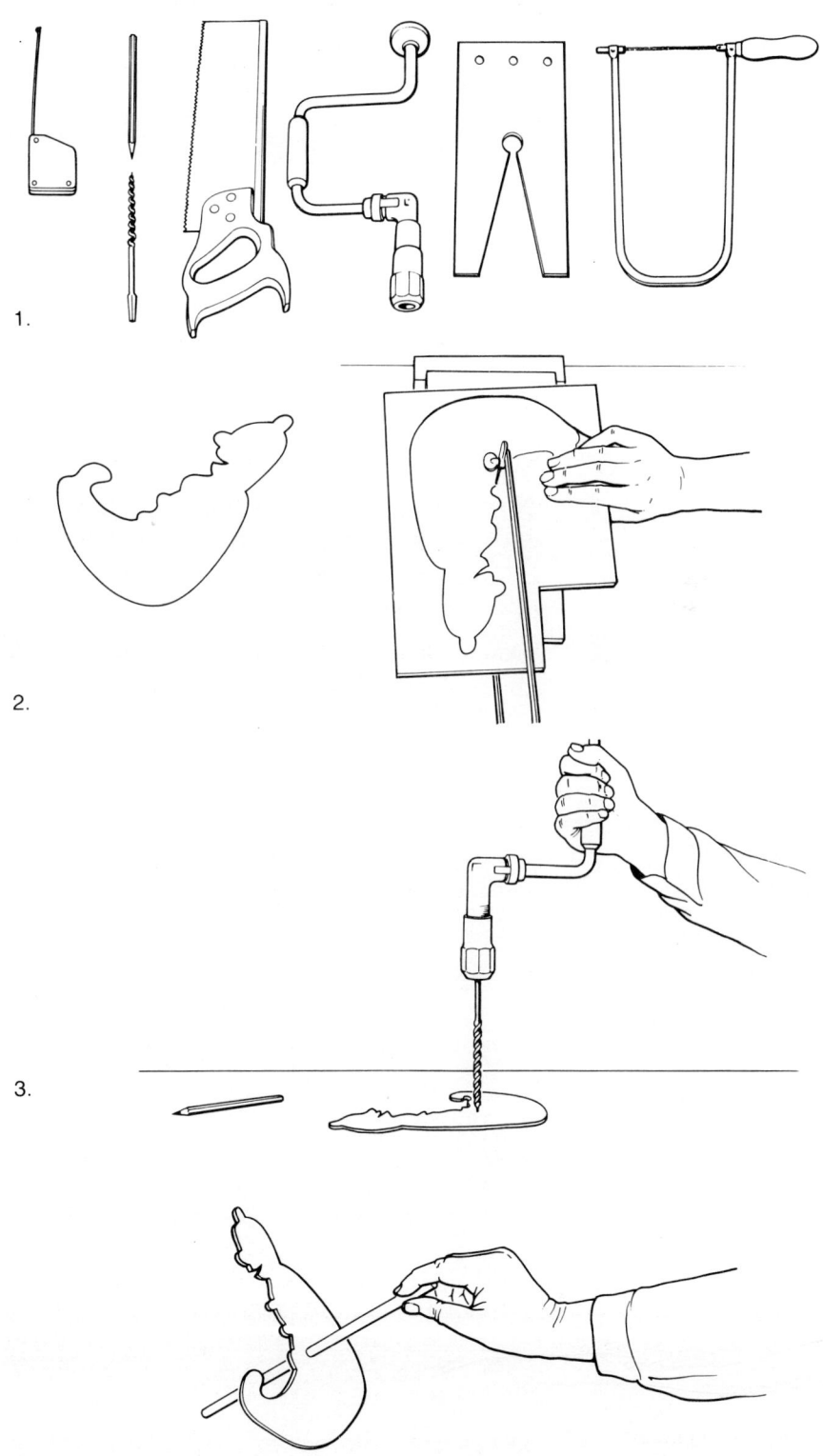

1.

2.

3.

Making the toy   4.

Task 4
I would consult textbooks for information on woodworking skills and the use of tools. The following are useful:

Building your own Wood Toys, R J DeCristoforo (Sterling)
The Essential Woodworker: Skills, Tools and Materials, R Wearing (Batsford)
A–Z Guide to Home Woodworking, F Sherlock (Constable)

Stage 3

Task 5
Next I will cut the main shape from plywood using a fretsaw, smoothing off the edges and surfaces to ensure safety. I will drill the hole for inserting the rod at the centre of gravity. It must be a tight fit.

Task 6
Now I will cut the dowelling to the required length, push through the hole, glue in place and wipe off the excess glue. The rod and shape must be exactly at right angles.

Task 7
Then I will decide what colour paints to use, what pattern if any to apply, the size of brush to use, the order of painting etc. Then I will paint the toy, leaving each coat to dry before applying the next layer, until a smooth finish is achieved. I will lightly sand with fine sandpaper between each coat.

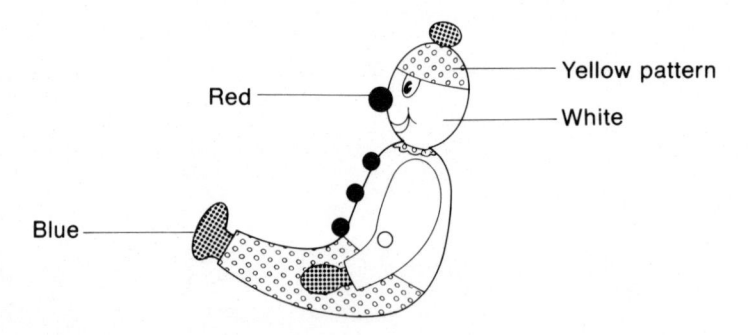

Colouring the toy

Task 8
Next I will drill small holes at each end of the rod, thread the string through and knot it in position.

Task 9
Making a loop at the centre point on the string, I will hang up the toy.

Task 10
To test that the toy works.

As I progress through my plan of action I must do everything detailed in Stage 4 on page 36.

Design brief 1

Stage 4 Critical appraisal and evaluation

When I checked the working of the toy I found that the string did not roll back up very easily. The cord I had used was quite stiff, waxed thread. I therefore changed this to softer finer string which worked much better. I did not need to make any further modifications.

The painting looked like an amateur job and could have been more carefully done, but it is cheerful and bright.

I then tried out the toy on Lesley. My original brief was to design and make a toy which would encourage her manipulative skills. The toy which I had made required very precise finger tip control to roll up the string on a slender rod, and the use of hand and eye co-ordinated movements. It would help to develop fine motor skills as Lesley played more and more with the toy. My report would therefore conclude that my brief had been successfully accomplished. I would continue to monitor the success of my toy by observing if Lesley:

* found the toy too easy or too difficult to work   * became bored with it   * showed interest in how and why it worked   * needed to use any other physical skills   * broke or wore out the toy in frequent use.

I would also make an accurate costing and compare it in value with a similar, shop-bought toy.

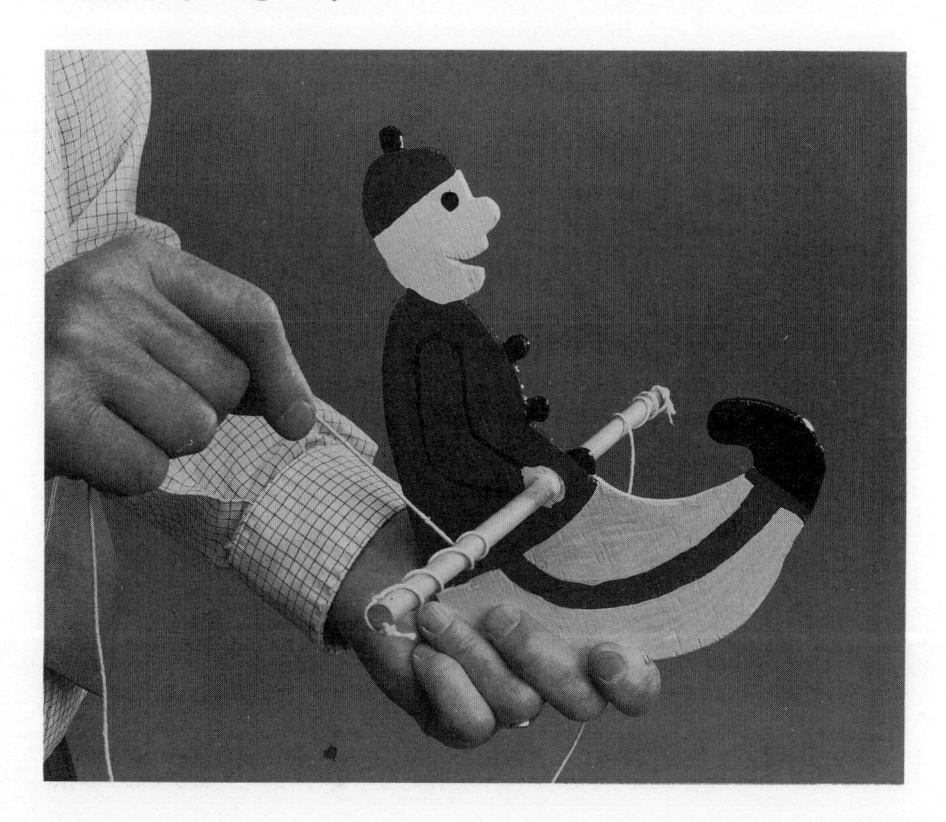

The finished toy

Stage 5
This consists of completing a Self Evaluation Report.

Self Evaluation Report	**Name**

Practical Item   Date started . . . .   completed . . . .

Design Brief

Aims of the brief

Skills used

New skills learnt

Assessment Objectives   Have I covered the Assessement Objectives with the correct weightings? (See explanation in Examination Terms)

Planning   Was this thorough, workable and applicable to the brief?
Generally was it — Very good ☐   good ☐   poor ☐

Improvements   Did I bother to make modifications and improvements?
Has this been a successful learning experience?
Have I enjoyed the tasks, or become bored or impatient? Why?

Is the outcome of my work the best answer to the initial problem or could I have made a better choice?

Extension work   Am I keen to do any extension work with this item and if so what form could this take?

Teacher's Comments   Date:

© Valda Reynolds and Stanley Thornes (Publishers) Ltd 1990, *Coursework Explained: Child Development*

Design brief 2

The Brief
To make something cheaply, which will enliven a baby's bedroom and be stimulating for a child. The problem to be solved is, how can I use several small, cheap remnants of cotton in bright primary colours to satisfy my design brief?

Stage 1
Exploration
I will consider the soft furnishings and decorations found in a nursery to help decide which would be suitable for my fabrics. I will use as sources of ideas:

> *Rooms to Grow up in,* Rosie Fisher (New Burlington Books)
> *Children's Rooms,* Mary Gilliatt (St. Michael)
> Catalogues from Habitat, BabyBoots, Mothercare etc.
> Magazines on parentcraft, sewing and craft.

IDEAS
1. Sheets, duvet cover
2. Cot bumpers
3. Curtains
4. Carry-cot covers
5. Changing mat
6. Cushions
7. Lampshade

Ideas of soft furnishings to make

Solving the problem
I will first consider the fabrics which I have, to assess their suitability. I have about 1 metre of cotton in royal blue, 1.5 metres of cotton with a teddy bear pattern, and a piece 2×0.5 metres of red cotton.
- Are all the fabrics of similar thickness, made from the same fibre?
- Do all the colours and the pattern look well together?
- Is the fabric soft enough for a baby; is it hard-wearing?
- Will the fabric wash well, do the colours run? I must carry out experiments to test how fast the colours are.
- Is the fabric very flammable? I must experiment for flame resistance.
- Does the fabric sew together and make up well?

I do not want to use fabric which frays badly, is tough to sew, is too harsh, does not wash or iron easily or would quickly wear out. It must be as safe in use as possible.

Then I will try to examine actual examples of these items in:

* specialist baby shops   * department stores   * the homes of parents and babies whom I know

I will be looking at:

* how they are made   * the designs   * ease of laundering
* fabrics used   * methods of decorating   * cost

Stage 2
Choice
Having carried out the research, my decision is to make a duvet cover and a cot bumper. With any leftover material I will make a cushion and hot water bottle cover.

Reasons for my choice:
- I wish to make the best use of my fabric as possible
- My sewing skills are limited and I could find curtains, blinds, a lampshade etc. very difficult. My chosen items will rely on the bright attractive colours for effect and the design can be simple
- The cushion and hot water bottle cover will give me the opportunity to use new craft skills such as quilting or appliqué if I wish.

Planning
There are several decisions to be made about the design and construction of the items:
- Probably a geometric pattern in the different fabrics will work best
- In joining the pieces together, what kind of seams and seam finishes should I use?
- I should consider the use of piping to define the edges of the duvet cover, bumper and cushion
- I must select suitable wadding or filling for the cot bumper
- What type of fasteners should I use on the various openings, and what methods are there of fixing the bumper to the cot safely?

My plan of action consists of seven tasks.

Design brief 2

Task 1
To select and draw out a design for both sides of the duvet cover. First I must note the standard measurements for a cot cover, then use graph paper to scale down the measurements. Then I will cut out various shapes in coloured paper (red, yellow, blue, patterned) and arrange them on the master plan until I find an attractive combination. The two sides of the cot cover can be different.

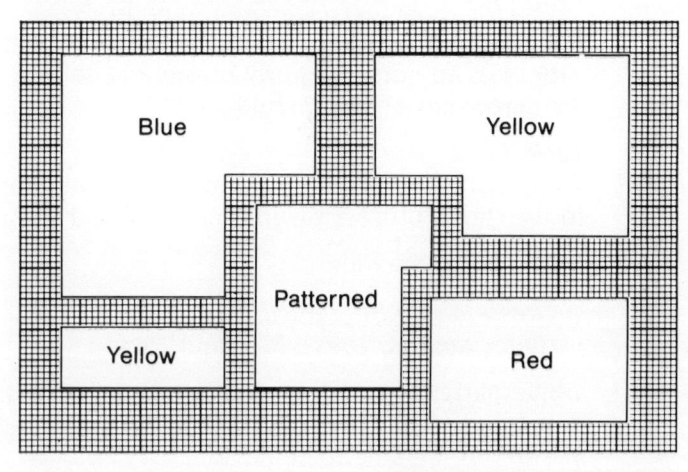

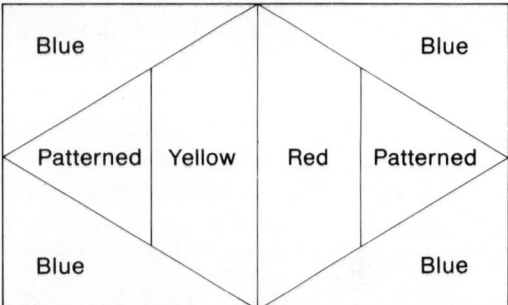

Design for duvet cover

I shall follow the same procedure for the cot bumper.

Task 2
To consider and select materials and processes to use.

Component	Possible Materials	Choice
Fabric	cotton: gingham, pique; polyester/cotton, nylon	polyester/cotton
Sewing thread	Sylko or Drima in matching colours	Drima
Other notions	soft piping cord; 3 cm width bias binding medium weight terylene wadding, rolled up for the cot bumper	
Fastenings	Duvet cover: buttons and button holes, press studs, popper tape, velcro, tying tapes.	popper tape or velcro

Reasons for Choices

Cotton is strong with a firm weave but can be quite difficult for laundering, and is also fairly expensive. Polyester/cotton is more crease resistant, washes and irons easily, is soft, comes in a good range of strong colours and patterns and is quite cheap. Nylon is slippery, non-absorbent, frays easily and is not as attractive.

Drima is a polyester thread suitable for polycotton fabrics.

Popper tape and velcro are quick and easy to use, can be obtained in a variety of colours, are fairly cheap and safe in use; tying tapes can be dangerous for a young child.

Task 3

To consult textbooks for information about choice of different processes to use, how to use a sewing machine and so on.

Useful books include:

> *Dressmaking Simplified,* Valerie Cook
> *Understanding Dress,* Margaret Picton

Vogue pattern no. 1514 gives detailed instructions for making similar items, but if you use a bought pattern it could reduce the number of marks you are able to achieve.

It is important to consider:
- which kind of seam to use: flat seam, overlaid seam, French seam
- methods of neatening seams: zig zag machine neatening, oversewing by hand, pinking with shears
- methods of applying piping: letting it into the seam, applying it by hand after making it up.

Stage 3

Task 4

To make up the items. This is my planned order of working.
Cut out my fabric pieces for the duvet cover according to my plan in Task 1. Do not forget to leave seam allowances.
Test the stitch of the sewing machine on scraps of fabric.
Join the fabric pieces together for each side of the quilt cover and neaten the seams.
Insert the popper tape or velcro.
Make up the piping.
Stitch the piping round the edges of one side of the cover.
Join the two cover sides together.
Final pressing and neatening.
For the cot bumper, cut two strips each of three colours 15 cm wide and 206 cm long.
Machine two strips together along one long edge and two short, turn and press.
Roll up wadding and push into the strip, tack raw edges together.
Attach third strip.

Design brief 2

Machine between each strip.
Machine stitch into three sections.
Attach tapes for holding bumper on to the cot; these should only be long enough to fit round the cot rails and should have velcro at each end for fastening.

Task 5
To assess the amount of materials left over to see if there is enough to make a custion and/or a hot water bottle cover.

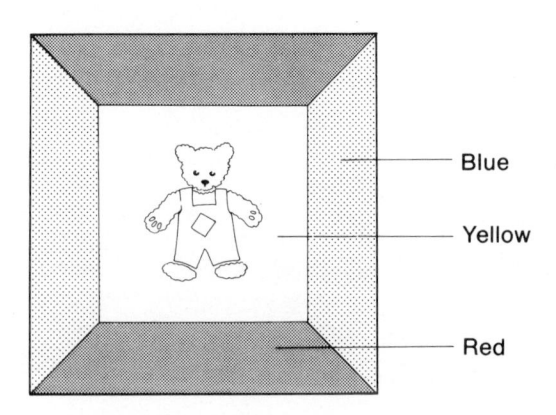

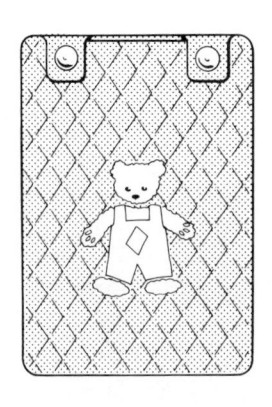

The cushion and hot water bottle cover

Cushion design
— Blue
— Yellow
— Red

Quilted hot water bottle cover

Task 6
To check each item made, for the quality of finish and safety. Check that the duvet cover fits the duvet, put it in the cot with the cot bumper. Make a critical appraisal and evaluation (on the same lines as those used for Design Brief 1 on page 37).

Task 7.
Complete a Self Evaluation Report, as on page 44.

Cot bumper, duvet cover and cushions

Practical items - further ideas

Design Briefs 1 and 2 give you extended guidelines for completing two items. They give help with identifying a need or problem, finding a solution, devising a course of action, carrying out the plan and then assessing the results. You can develop the following ideas along similar lines. The first two items are linked to an investigational study (see Component 3).

Childhood problems connected with feeding and sleeping

Ideas of toys to choose from

Topsy-turvy doll

Doll's cot

Identification of specific problem.
Miranda is two-and-a-half years old and does not like to be left in her bed to go to sleep at night. What toy could I design and make which could help to solve this problem?

I could make this Topsy–Turvy doll which is a smiling, sleeping doll at one end, wearing a nightdress and a wide-awake doll at the other end. I could also make a simple bed for the sleeping doll to use. These items could be made very cheaply from a cardboard box, left-over fabric, lace and felt. It would be very attractive for a child; also strong and safe. They would be used to encourage the child to 'put dolly to bed' when she herself goes to bed.

Encouraging children to look after their possessions

Identification of specific problem.
Darren shares a bedroom with his younger brother. How can he store his toys and games cheaply, neatly and efficiently?

Practical items - further ideas

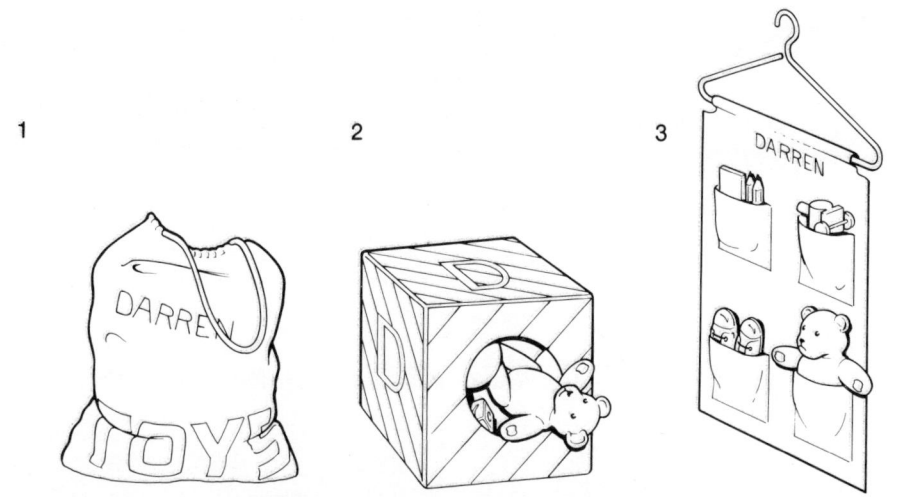

1 2 3

More designs to choose from

Some ideas might be:
- a strong toy bag made from denim or TVP with his name on
- a strong cardboard box, covered with thick wallpaper or padded fabric, to store his toys and games
- a door hanging with several different pockets for individual items.

Any of these items could be completed very cheaply, the main aims being child appeal, strength and safety.

They would meet the criteria needs for efficient storage, encouraging children to care for their own possessions.

The following is an item linked to a child study (see Component 1).

Leon's hand/eye co-ordination

The child being studied is Leon who is three-and-a-half years old. The special development area being applied is hand/eye coordination, including size, shape and colour recognition.

Identification of a specific need.

I need to plan, develop and make an educational toy which will help Leon develop the skills of shape, size and colour recognition, at the same time helping him with manipulative skills.

The drop-in jigsaw puzzles are very simple; different sizes, shapes and colours of animals can be used. Use 9 mm plywood because it is strong and easily cut with a fretsaw; the toy would be safe and cheap. Shape dominoes provide an interesting and instructive game for a three to four year old. The dominoes are made from 9 mm plywood, 300 mm × 150 mm, making a set of 28. Six basic shapes must be chosen, e.g. heart, circle, triangle, star, diamond, square; each shape to be a different colour. The shapes could be raised and given different textures, so extending the project to make it suitable for a visually handicapped child.

Practical items

Shape dominoes game

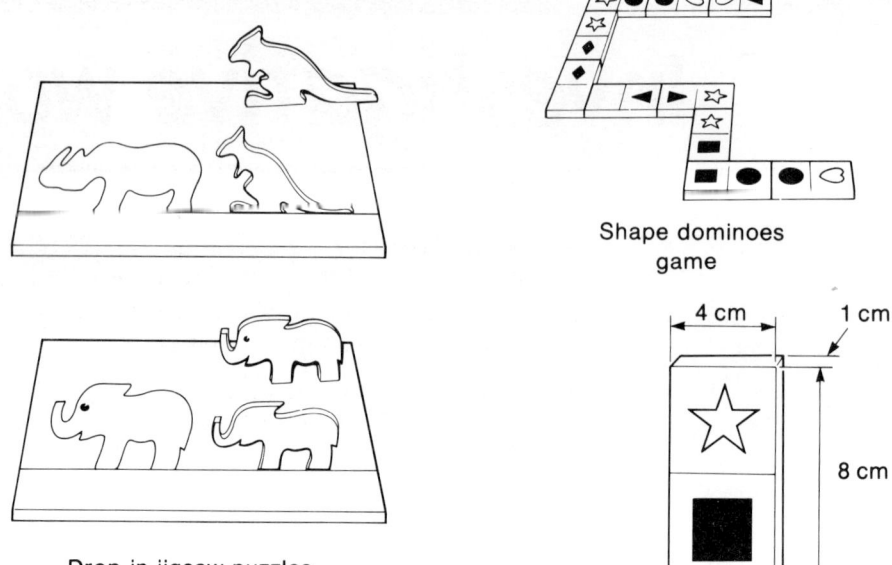

Games which could be made

Drop-in jigsaw puzzles

The last example is for a free choice item linked to the Food aspect of Home Economics.

Healthy eating project
Small children often go through periods of food refusal and it is tempting for carers to give in and feed them only the foods they like, which can result in an unhealthy, unbalanced diet.

Identification of a specific need.
What is needed is a teaching aid which will encourage a child to select healthy foods and reject less healthy ones.

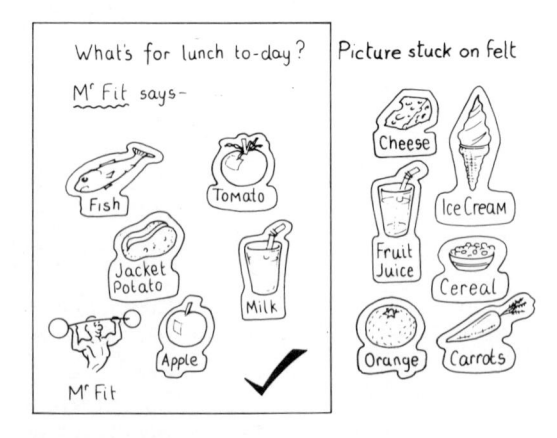

Fuzzy felt picture cards

The fuzzy felt picture cards shown in the illustration could be produced quite cheaply from thin felt stuck on card. A selection of pictures of food, mounted on felt, would form the other component. The child would be encouraged to select healthy foods for his meals.

COMPONENT THREE

Investigative work

Guidelines

The other practical component included in the syllabuses of most of the examining boards is the Investigational Study (or Studies). This can be one of the most difficult of the internally assessed coursework components in which to obtain high marks, very often because the candidate does not clearly recognise what is required.

The investigational study must involve practical research into a chosen area(s); candidates must use a wide range of investigational techniques, and different ways of presenting results and conclusions.

Board requirements differ.

		Mark allocation
NISEC	Choose 1 from 4 given assignments	40%
Southern		20%
Welsh	Choose 1 from 7 given areas	20%
MEG	1 free choice from the syllabus	15%
LEAG	2 free choices from the syllabus	10%
NEA	None	

(Correct at the time of going to press)

The information given in your syllabus is important and includes details of:
- the compulsory list of topics to choose from (if there is one)
- the subject content, and the age limit of the child; if you go beyond this age limit or outside the subject content your investigation may be unacceptable or penalised
- what your investigation should contain and how the marks are allocated for each part
- the length of the investigation; an approximate number of words may be given
- the importance of relating the work to the common themes and common elements. Some syllabuses make this relationship a compulsory factor
- investigative techniques and methods of presentation you could use
- the skills you will need to use
- teacher intervention. Some boards deduct marks on a sliding scale for small, medium or large amounts of help received from your teacher.

Study the following points as they will help you in your work.
- Ask for teacher support and guidance on anything which you do not understand.

- Check if there is a suggested length of time which your study should take.
- See if there are any special instructions about the type and size of paper to use, the cover, headings, method of presentation etc.
- Select suitable resources such as: information packs from manufacturers and voluntary agencies; articles from magazines or newspapers; TV and radio programmes; leaflets, booklets and textbooks.
- Use your support material and refer to it in your work, but don't include it as unrelated material or quote straight from it.
- Include a list of the books and resources which you have used.
- Use a wide variety of investigative techniques, e.g. observation and observation sheets, surveys, experiments, interviews, questionnaires and testing.
- Use a wide choice of methods of recording information, e.g. graphs, diagrams, photographs, illustrations, samples, computer programs, drawings, tape recordings, maps, tally charts, bar and pie charts. Many of these techniques and methods are to be found in *Finding Out About Child Development,* Valda Reynolds (Stanley Thornes).
- Devise and use a flow chart to explain your plan of action and evaluation charts for final analysis.
- Always justify and give reasons for your choices of action.
- Keep a record of everything you do, including things that go wrong and adjustments which have to be made.
- Don't pad your work out with irrelevant, unrelated information, just to give it extra length. Quality, not quantity, is what matters.
- Avoid using whole collections of completed questionnaires. Just put in one as an example and then an analysis of your results.
- The area you choose to investigate should not be too wide. Select a problem or situation to investigate it in depth, not breadth, e.g. an investigation into 'choosing toys' could be narrowed down into a few stated categories.
- If your work is very brief, untidily presented and does not follow the criteria, your marks will be low.

When your work is complete, review it and ask yourself these questions:
- Could I make any improvements?
- Has my work been assessed up to date?
- Have I included everything in my plan?
- Does any irrelevant material need to be removed?
- Am I satisfied that I have done my very best work?

Planning your investigative work

The flow chart on page 55 illustrates the order in which to complete your work and the areas where marks will be allocated.

The sample investigational studies which follow are not complete. They are meant as a guide to help you work out your own ideas and methods.

Guidelines

```
┌─────────────────────────────────────────────────────────────┐
│ Select an area of study (free choice or board selection)    │
│ which interests you.                                        │
└─────────────────────────────────────────────────────────────┘
                              ↓
┌─────────────────────────────────────────────────────────────┐
│ State the subject area you have chosen, giving reasons for  │
│ your selection.                                             │
└─────────────────────────────────────────────────────────────┘
                              ↓
┌─────────────────────────────────────────────────────────────┐
│ Identify the situation or problem you are investigating,    │
│ possibly in the form of a question.                         │
└─────────────────────────────────────────────────────────────┘
                              ↓
┌─────────────────────────────────────────────────────────────┐
│ Consider a range of methods of obtaining information and    │
│ the techniques which you can use. Select and justify your   │
│ choices.                                                    │
└─────────────────────────────────────────────────────────────┘
                              ↓
┌─────────────────────────────────────────────────────────────┐
│ Make a detailed plan of your course of action.              │
└─────────────────────────────────────────────────────────────┘
                              ↓
┌─────────────────────────────────────────────────────────────┐
│ Decide how to record your work and present your results;    │
│ give reasons.                                               │
└─────────────────────────────────────────────────────────────┘
                              ↓
┌─────────────────────────────────────────────────────────────┐
│ Carry out your course of action, making any necessary       │
│ modifications.                                              │
└─────────────────────────────────────────────────────────────┘
                              ↓
┌─────────────────────────────────────────────────────────────┐
│ Record your work; justify any modifications of plan.        │
└─────────────────────────────────────────────────────────────┘
                              ↓
┌─────────────────────────────────────────────────────────────┐
│ Analyse and interpret your results, making reasoned         │
│ conclusions.                                                │
└─────────────────────────────────────────────────────────────┘
                              ↓
┌─────────────────────────────────────────────────────────────┐
│ Evaluate your work; give a critical appraisal of your       │
│ planning, organisation and presentation.                    │
└─────────────────────────────────────────────────────────────┘
                              ↓
┌─────────────────────────────────────────────────────────────┐
│ Suggest how your work could have been improved and          │
│ identify any further areas of work.                         │
└─────────────────────────────────────────────────────────────┘
```

© Valda Reynolds and Stanley Thornes (Publishers) Ltd 1990, *Coursework Explained: Child Development*

Investigation 1: Community provision for the under-fives

The Brief
Do the social and educational provisions in my neighbourhood provide adequately for the under-fives?

Reasons for choosing this brief
I live in an area where there is a high proportion of young children, some of them from overcrowded, deprived home conditions. I think that the facilities available are inadequate in range and choice. I would like to compare these provisions with that of another area.

Resources and information gathering
I will need to find out:
- what statutory and voluntary provisions are generally available in this country
- who provides and finances these provisions
- which of them are available in my neighbourhood
- why there is not a larger choice
- what parents and carers think of the choice available
- how we compare with a neighbouring town
- if it is a satisfactory situation or if it could be improved
- how the situation could be improved.

To obtain this information I can contact any of the following.
- The Social Services Department of the local authority who must register all provisions for the under-fives.
- The public library which should have lists of leisure and educational provision.
- The Citizen's Advice Bureau (CAB).
- The phone book and Yellow Pages.
- The leisure centre for activities for the under-fives.
- The public library. Do they hold storytelling sessions or have a toy library?
- The town hall to ask about local amenities and obtain a map showing where public parks, recreation grounds, adventure parks, play areas are to be found.
- The Educational Department about educational facilities for the under-fives.
- The local branch of the Pre-school Playgroups Association (PPA) for local information.

I should also enquire about community centres, drop-in centres, family centres and centres for Asian and ethnic minority groups, voluntary organisations such as Meet-a-Mum Association (MAMA), mother and toddler groups, church groups for mothers with young children, Barnados, National Children's Home (NCH), and Church of England Children's Society (who often run voluntary nurseries).

Investigation 1: Community provision for the under-fives

I can look for advertisements and information about activities for children, check local swimming pools, dance and exercise classes, riding schools etc., to see if they hold sessions specially for parent and child.

I can use books such as:

The Sunday Times Self Help Directory, ed. Gillie, Price and Robinson (Granada Publishing)
Maternity Rights Handbook, Evans and Durward (Penguin)
Open University Community Education Pack 'Finding Out' (Open University Press)

I can interview:

* parents and carers * playgroup leaders and nursery school teachers * a local councillor * public library official * leisure centre official * small children who use the facilities * members of community groups and ethnic minority groups

I can observe:

* playgroups and nursery class sessions * group meetings of MAMA * mother and toddler groups * children's activities at the public library * swimming sessions etc.

This information gathering will take a lot of time and work and could be expensive; I must therefore be selective. When dealing with people I must be very sensitive to their needs and feelings.

Methods of recording information
There will be a mass of information which will need collating and recording accurately and concisely. I shall use (if possible) maps, drawings, photographs, original notes, surveys, questionnaires, charts and tape recorded interviews.

Plan of Action

Task 1
At school, home and in the public library collect information from books, leaflets, information packs, magazines, local newspapers etc. Send for other information from voluntary agencies, social services, official bodies (as detailed above).

Task 2
Visit the Town Hall, Education Office, public library, CAB etc. for information about available facilities and their whereabouts.

Task 3
Produce maps to show what is available and where it is. Two maps will be needed, one to show social/recreational facilities, one for educational facilities.

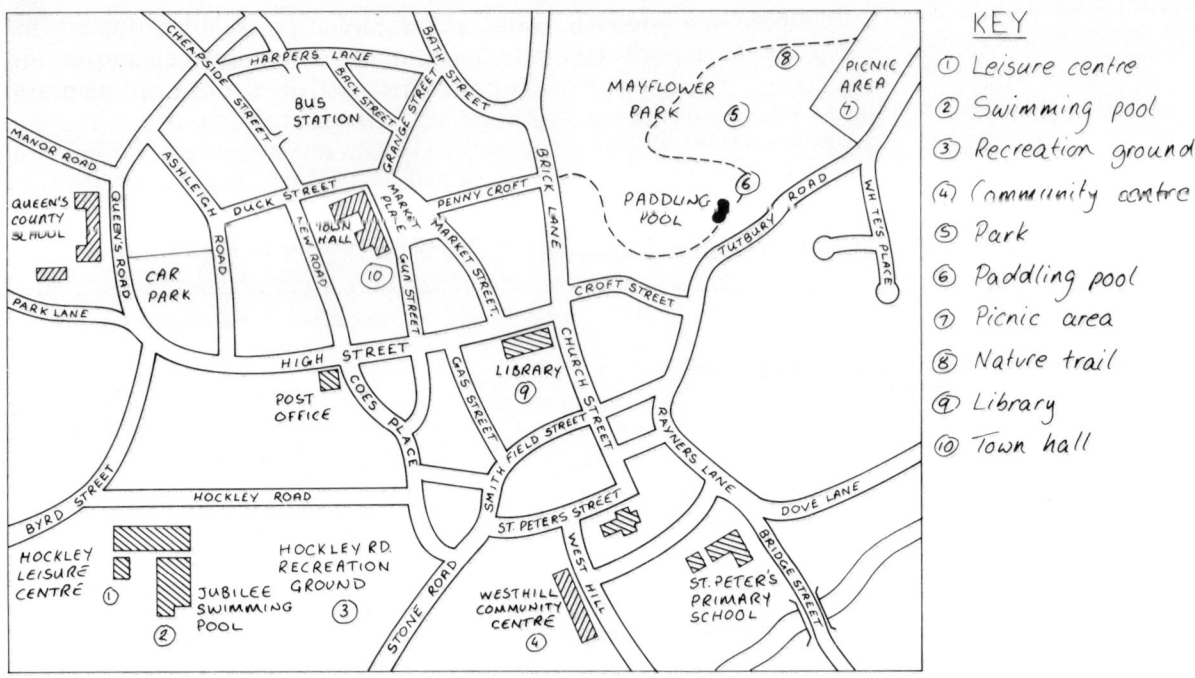

KEY
① Leisure centre
② Swimming pool
③ Recreation ground
④ Community centre
⑤ Park
⑥ Paddling pool
⑦ Picnic area
⑧ Nature trail
⑨ Library
⑩ Town hall

Leisure and social activities

Task 4

Prepare sets of questionnaires, interview leads, observational sheets etc. This is an example of the kind of questions I would ask parents taking small children to the mother and toddler group at the church hall.
- What is the purpose of this group?
- How long have you been attending?
- What types of activity take place?
- Is it well organised?
- Do the children play well together?
- Are toys and games arranged?
- Do you have interesting speakers?
- Are you happy with the premises?
- Could you suggest any improvements?

These are sample questions I would ask a playgroup leader.
- Is your playgroup popular?
- Is there a waiting list?
- Do you involve parents in your activities?
- Do you receive a grant from the local council?
- Do you welcome children with minor handicaps?
- What proportion of children from ethnic minority groups (e.g. from Bangladeshi, Indian, Chinese or Afro-Caribbean backgrounds) do you have?
- Are most of your children from poor or wealthy backgrounds or is there a mixture?
- Do you think more playgroups and nursery school provision should be made?

Investigation 1: Community provision for the under-fives

I will attend a storytelling session at the public library, swimming for the under-fives at the leisure centre and a movement and dance session for 'the tinies' to find out how popular these activities are. I can also ask about the socio-economic groups who attend and how expensive the sessions are. Why do parents take their children there and what they hope to get out of it?

The following is an observation sheet to use at the local park.

Observations	Yes	No	Excellent	Satisfactory	Poor
Is the park popular with all ages of children?					
Is it in a safe location?					
Is it easily accessible by bus?					
Is there a large enough car park?					
How would you describe the toilet facilities?					
Is drinking water available?					
Are reasonably priced refreshments available?					
Is there a good range of rides and activities?					
Are they well maintained?					
How would you describe the play area surfaces?					
Are small children safe from dogs, strangers, older children, traffic?					
How would you describe the safety planning?					
Is there a play leader?					
Are there sufficient wardens?					

Observations made by children and parents (taped if possible)

© Valda Reynolds and Stanley Thornes (Publishers) Ltd 1990, *Coursework Explained: Child Development*

This is a sample interview with a local councillor.
- Why does this area compare quite badly with others in providing facilities for the under-fives? (Show him/her the information so far gathered.)
- Why are so many expensive activities not subsidised?
- Are there any plans to improve the range of facilities?
- Would you care for a copy of my survey to bring to the attention of the council?

Task 5
I will try to find information about an area nearby where facilities differ. I will then compare the range and standard of facilities offered in both areas and try to discover reasons for the differences. These reasons could include:
- different funding by the district and town councils
- smaller or greater demand by users
- predominance of different socio/economic groups
- differing parental interest in organising and pressing for more and better facilities.

Task 6
I will carry out my plan of action making any necessary alterations. When recording my work I will use all the information I have gathered, analysing it and only including what is relevant.

Task 7 Evaluation
a) How did I find my investigation brief?
   too wide ☐   too restricting ☐   just right ☐
   Give reasons.
b) Did I collect together sufficient information to work with? Were my methods of collecting information varied and efficient? What other methods could I have used successfully?
c) Was the planning for my course of action totally successful? How could it have been improved?
d) What are my impressions of the finished result?
   Totally satisfied ☐   Could be improved with more effort ☐
   Very unsatisfactory because:
e) What about the time spent on this component?
   too much ☐   insufficient ☐
f) Have I covered the syllabus requirements fully?

Investigation 1: Community provision for the under-fives

Task 8
I will complete a Self Evaluation Report like the one below.

Self Evaluation Report	**Name**	
Investigation	Date started	Date finished
Time Management	I used my time: well ☐ quite well ☐ inefficiently ☐	
Work organisation	I was well organised throughout ☐ I was reasonably organised ☐ I was very disorganised ☐	
Contact with others	I approached others with confidence and sensitivity ☐ I was rather unsure of myself ☐ I improved as I went along ☐	
Interest	I enjoyed this work and maintained my interest throughout ☐ I was interested at first, but lost interest part way through ☐ I very soon lost interest and wished I had chosen another topic ☐	
Reasons	These are my reasons for certain of my self evaluation statements:	
Extension	Could this topic be usefully extended and developed? E.g., investigating the health facilities for under-fives in my area.	
Teacher's Comments		Date

© Valda Reynolds and Stanley Thornes (Publishers) Ltd 1990, *Coursework Explained: Child Development*

Investigation 2: Clothing for the baby and child

The Brief
Find out about clothing designed for children starting school, for physically handicapped children and for premature babies.

Reasons for choosing this brief
I am interested in design and fabrics. I would like to investigate what clothing is available for these special need categories and how parents could adapt and produce garments themselves.

I must consider the purpose of clothing. For children the main purposes are protection, warmth in cold weather and modesty. I must also consider essentials such as:

* washability   * cost   * durability   * safety   * child appeal
* functional design   * fibres and fabrics.

I must apply these considerations to the categories I have chosen to investigate.

Resources and information gathering
To obtain general information on children's clothing, I can look through catalogues such as Kays, Littlewoods; specialist catalogues such as Mothercare, Boots, Oh/One/Oh!, Young Additions, Clothkits; magazines, for special articles on clothing e.g. *Practical Parenting, Under Five*.

For information on *premature babies'* clothing, I can send for catalogues from Babycare, Harrington's Low Birthweight Range, Poppers, Premgems, Tiddlywinks, Tiny Trends. Copley's have low birthweight knitting patterns; Style have a dungaree or dress pattern suitable for a 1.4 kg (3 lb) baby.

I can request information leaflets from the premature babies support group 'Nippers' and the National Childbirth Trust.

I can look for knitting and sewing patterns for dolls' clothing. For information on clothing for physical handicaps, I can send for the Wizzywear catalogue and information from the Spastic Society.

I can use books such as:

Finding Out About Textiles, Gillian Jones (Stanley Thornes Ltd)
All About Fabrics, Stephanie Holland (Oxford University Press)
Basic Fashion Design, J. Ireland (Batsford)
You and Your Premature Baby, Barbara Glover/Christine Hodson (Sheldon Press)

I can visit Mothercare, who offer a range of 55 cm (22") clothing suitable for a 1.8 kg (4 lb) baby, and market stalls, which sometimes supply small sizes. Also I can visit specialist children's clothing shops to look at prices, styles and fabrics; infant schools to see what children are wearing;

Investigation 2: Clothing for the baby and child

playgroups and schools which cater for handicapped children; shops which supply fabrics and yarns.

I can interview parents and children to record their opinions; the clothing buyer at Mothercare or other specialist shops; the parent of a handicapped child to discover any clothing problems; a nurse at the Special Baby Unit (SBU) to find out how they cope.

Methods of recording information

First I will give brief general points about children's clothing, then I will divide my work into the three categories. I will carry out some experimental work on testing of fibres and fabrics, and make some comparison charts on the methods of laundering fabrics, buying garments cheaply, the difference in price between homemade and shop-bought garments. I will survey shops and markets and produce questionnaires and information sheets. This will give me a wide variety of investigative techniques allowing me to produce concise, interesting work.

Plan of Action

My plan of action falls into eight tasks.

Task 1

I will assemble general information about children's clothing, and make a collection of fibres, yarns and fabrics. Then I will begin to divide my

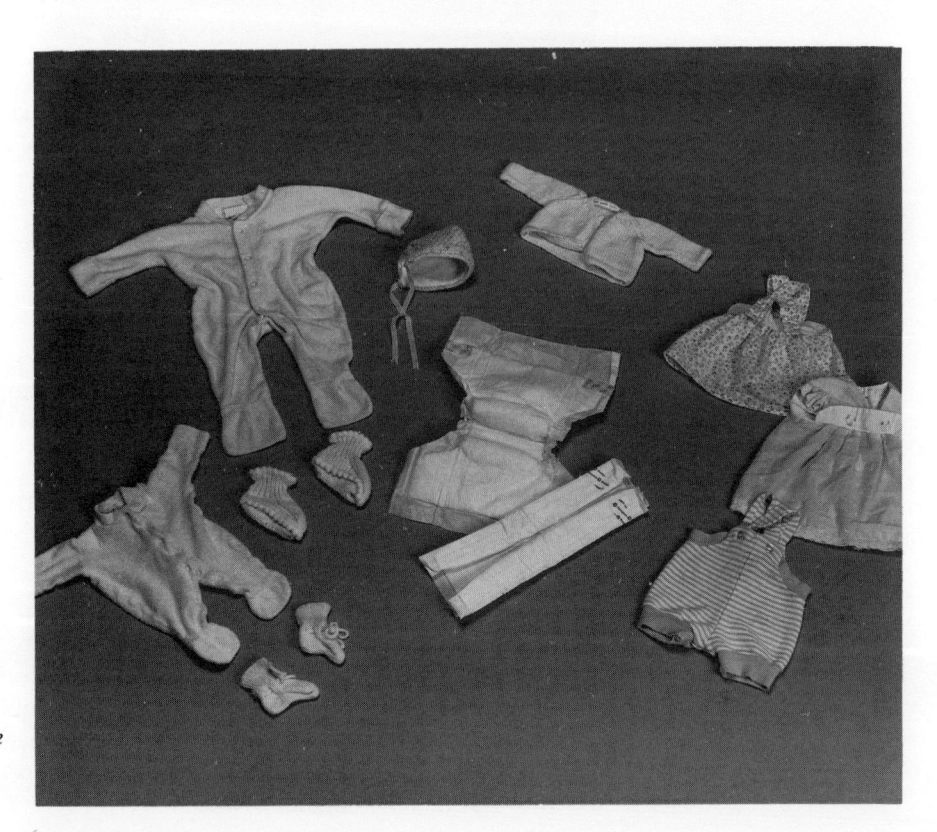

Clothes for premature babies. The larger nappy, stretch-suit and bootees are for a new-born, full-term baby.

information into the three categories. My information sheets (see examples) will show the styles available commercially, how styles can be adapted, special points about each of the three categories, and samples of fibres, yarns and fabrics and their suitability, with reasons.

Information Sheet — 1. Clothing for premature babies

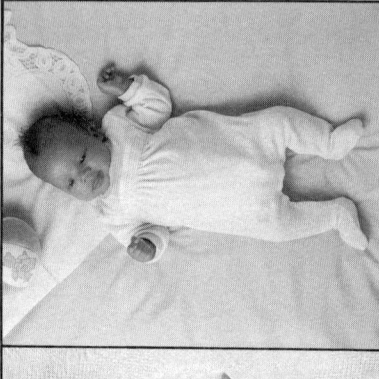

Stretch suits must be very tiny, made from soft, stretchy material for comfort. Cardigans can quickly be knitted from fine, soft wool using a special pattern.

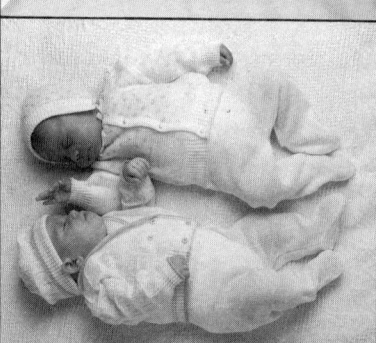

Do not use ready-made doll's clothes; they are usually badly made, too tight at the neck and in the arms, and wash badly. Nylon thread can prick the baby, and can be dangerous.

A selection from Mothercare, size 50–55, suitable for a 1.8 kg (4 lb) baby. Made from cotton and nylon mix. Price range £4.50–£5.99.

Special baby units may have garments which open to allow for feeding tubes etc and close with velcro strips.

Task 2

I will visit my nearest large town to survey the shops and the market. I will visit Mothercare, Marks and Spencer, Woolworths, Boots, Children's World, the market, fabric and yarn shops.

I will obtain information about ready-made clothing for each of my three categories; patterns and fabrics and yarns for making at home; costs, range of selection, helpfulness of staff etc.

I will try to interview a member of staff to ask:

* which are the most popular ranges of clothing
* if they have much demand for tiny clothes for premature babies
* if all the clothes are washable
* what safety measures are emphasised
* if they stock clothing specially for handicapped children
* whether they would take special orders

Investigation 2: Clothing for the baby and child

Information Sheet — 2. Clothing for a handicapped child

Styles
Very generously cut, lots of gathers and fullness; openings — full length or velcro; very fashionable with lots of decorative features.
Designed with child appeal.

Fabrics
Bright, fun patterns, hard wearing, washable, comfortable.

Cost
Quite expensive (*eg.* unisex dungarees £24.99) but well designed and attractive.

Task 3
To carry out some experimental work. Some examples follow.

Experiment 1:
To compare the absorbency of various fibres and fabrics.

Children perspire a lot when involved in energetic activities. If the clothing they are wearing does not readily absorb moisture they will feel cold, clammy and uncomfortable.

I will test:
  natural fibres: cotton and wool
  artificial fibres: nylon and polyester
  a blend of fibres: polycotton

Procedure:
  1 Select pieces of fabric of similar size and thickness, made from the fibres listed above.
  2 Place each piece of fabric in a foil dish.
  3 Pour in a measured amount of water.
  4 Leave for fifteen minutes.
  5 Drain the water from each dish and measure each amount.
  6 The water drained off will show how much was not absorbed by the fabric, so a comparison can be made.
  7 Graph the results.
  8 Record the conclusions.

Experiment 2:
To show the washability of various children's garments and how this is influenced by style and fabric.

It must be possible to quickly and easily wash and iron children's clothing. It should preferably be machine washable. Colours should not run and the fabric should not shrink, go hard or 'milll up'.

Procedure:
1 Select various children's garments e.g. a baby's stretch suit; a hand-knitted woollen jumper; a wool interlock vest; navy blue cord trousers; track suit; nylon party dress; polycotton, laced-trimmed nightdress; cotton socks; multi-coloured acrylic cardigan. These should be of varying quality, from various manufacturers and shops e.g. Mothercare, Ladybird.
2 Handwash the garments, following the care label instructions.
3 Note any difficulties such as resistant stains, colour running.
4 Hang out to dry; note any tendency to stretch or lose shape.
5 Iron the garments, noting the ease or difficulty and amount of skill required.
6 Allocate a mark out of ten for each process.
7 Assess the washability of each garment and any problems which may have occurred.
8 Record the conclusions and recommendations.

Task 4
I will undertake some consumer studies.

1 Comparative costs. I will carry out a comparative study for each of my three categories to find out how much could be saved by making garments at home rather than buying them in shops. For example, in each category I could compare the following.
   □ school clothing:
       a hand-knitted pullover and a hand-made pinafore dress compared with ones from shops
   □ clothing for handicapped children:
       a hand-made protective bib and a unisex shirt compared with shop-bought ones
   □ premature baby clothing:
       a hand-knitted matinee coat, mittens, hat and bootees compared with shop-bought ones.
2 I will survey various commercial outlets e.g. department stores, specialist shops, market stalls, catalogues, 'seconds' shops, to compare the prices of the same or similar garments. I will suggest cheap methods of obtaining children's clothing, e.g. jumble sales, hand-me-downs, borrowing from friends, charity shops, shop sales.

Investigation 2: Clothing for the baby and child

3 I will do a consumer survey of parents to find out which manufactured clothing gives the best value for money. These are some sample questions:

Where do you usually obtain clothing for your children?
  Mothercare ☐   Marks and Spencer ☐   Woolworths ☐
  Debenhams ☐   catalogue ☐   market ☐   others:

Why do you do so?
  better quality ☐   original designs ☐   cheaper ☐
  better made ☐   attractive ☐   impulse ☐
  can try on at home ☐

Do you look for sale bargains?
  yes ☐   no ☐

If not, why not?

Task 5
I shall visit an infant and a primary school to observe what children wear to go to school.

Clothes for school

I will produce a selection chart (see example) to show to children and parents, so they can make a choice of garments, and observe the differences between what children and parents prefer.

I will ask a sample selection of parents certain questions, e.g.
☐ Do you make any of your children's clothes?
☐ Are most children's garments too expensive?
☐ Should all children's clothing be free of VAT?

Task 6
I will carry out my plan of action making any necessary modifications and recording my results in a variety of ways. I will make a final check to ensure that I have not included irrelevant or unacknowledged information.

Task 7
Make an evaluation (as for Investigation 1, see page 60).

Task 8
Complete a Self Evaluation Report (see format on page 61).

Investigative work - further ideas

Community provisions statutory and voluntary

The Brief
To assess the efficiency of the sources of help and guidance available for prospective parents.

Divide the investigation into the following parts and discover the help and guidance available for each.

Pre-conceptional help and guidance
- medical: family doctor, geneticist, health centre, family planning clinic
- family/church: advice on family values and parental roles

Help and guidance during pregnancy
- financial: DSS, voluntary societies
- medical: GP, specialists, health visitor, midwife, pre-natal clinics, hospitals, maternity units
- housing and environment: local council, town hall
- voluntary: CAB, consumer associations, single parent family organisations, National Childbirth Trust, La Leche League etc.

Visit some of these services; interview officials, medical personnel, voluntary workers. Discover some of the strengths and weaknesses of the help available. Draw conclusions from the information gathered, to assess the efficiency of the statutory and voluntary services available.

Safety in the home and the environment

The Brief
What are the major causes of accidents to children in the home and garden and how can homes be made adequately safe for children?

Accidents in the home are the commonest cause of death of children over one year old. Four British children are accidently killed every day in the home and more than a million children attend hospital emergency departments each year because of accidents at home.

For this assignment, investigate the statistics dealing with accidents to children, analyse these to discover the major causes of accidents and then offer solutions to how they may be prevented.

Divide the home into major accident zones e.g. kitchen, stairs, garden, and identify the types of accidents which commonly occur.

Child and parent magazines, safety organisations such as RoSPA, shops such as Boots and Mothercare, all produce literature and/or gadgets connected with making the home safe for children. Some of these devices could be tested and assessed. Home safety questionnaires for parents with young children and a home safety booklet could be devised.

Other interesting areas upon which to base ideas for investigative work include:

- Feeding the under fives: establishing a healthy eating pattern; ways to avoid excess consumption of sugar, salt, fats.
- Babies with special needs: genetic testing, infant testing, premature babies, SCBUs, cot deaths.
- Voluntary support groups for the single parent. Who organises them? What are their aims? How good are they?
- Multiple births: factors which cause twins, triplets etc. Identical and non-identical twins; dealing with twins and triplets.
- Outdoor activities for children; organised and informal games and play; parks and adventure playgrounds; large scale toys; safety and design.

Syllabuses and past examination papers

There are six examining groups which set GCSE courses in Child Development. If you wish to obtain your own copy of a syllabus or back copies of examination papers, ask your teacher which examining group is being used and then write or phone for information.

London, East Anglian Group
Publications Dept
The Lindens
139 Lexden Road
COLCHESTER
Essex CO3 3RL

Midland Examining Group
The WMEB
Norfolk House
Smallbrook Queensway
BIRMINGHAM
B5 4NJ

Welsh Joint Education Committee
Publications Dept
245 Western Avenue
CARDIFF
CF5 2YK

Southern Examining Group
Publications Dept
Stag Hill House
GUILDFORD
GU2 5XY

North Regional Examinations Board
Wheatfield Road
Westerhope
Newcastle upon Tyne
NE5 5JZ

Northern Ireland Schools Exam. Council
Publications Dept
Beechill House
Beechill Road
BELFAST
BT8 4RD

Syllabuses cost about 65p–£1.25
Back papers cost about 40p–50p

Video suppliers

The video films mentioned in this book can be obtained from the following suppliers.

Child Behaviour — You
Guild Sound and Vision Ltd
6 Joyce Road
Peterborough PE1 5YB

Social Growth in Infants
Resources Section
Audio Visual Centre
University of Newcastle upon Tyne
Newcastle upon Tyne NE1 3RU

Baby and Co. 2
Community Education
Yorkshire TV Centre
Leeds LS3 1JS

The Child's World
ILEA Learning Resources Branch
TV and Publishing Centre
Thackery Road
London SW8 3TB

The First Ten Months
Oxford Educational Resources Ltd
197 Botley Road
Oxford OX2 0HE

Family Matters (Parts 5 and 6)
Concord Films Council Ltd
201 Felixtowe Road
Ipswich
Suffolk IP3 9BJ

The First Years of Life
LMSO
The Open University
PO Box 188
Walton Hall
Milton Keynes
Buckinghamshire MK7 6DH

Index

Accepted norms   viii, 6, 7, 8, 10–12, 27
Accidents to children   69
Assessment objectives   viii, xi, 13, 32

Clothing – baby and child   62–8
Common: elements   viii, 1, 32, 35
        themes   32
Community provisions   69
Confidentiality   1
Creativity   3, 27–30, 31

Design   33–6
Discrimination   18

Emotional disturbance   21

Family: nuclear   9
       extended   9
Forward planning   viii, 8, 15, 24, 27, 34

Hand/eye co-ordination   6, 37, 51

Investigations   56, 62, 69

Language development   3, 18, 31

Manipulative skills   ix, 6, 27, 30, 37, 51
Marking allocation   ix, 2, 33, 53
Marking scheme   ix, 2
Mark weighting   ix, xii, 32
Mobility skills   8

Moderation   32
Mother and Toddler groups   56–61

Nursery school   57

Observational studies   ix, 1–2, 8–31

Physical: co-ordination   3, 37
        milestones   5
        development   8, 10
        handicap   16, 51, 58, 62–4
Play   3, 15–26, 31, 56–60, 70
   solitary   18, 20, 21, 23
   parallel   20, 23
   group   20, 21, 23
Playgroup   15–26, 56–60
Practical work   37, 45, 50
Pre-conceptual period   31
Protective clothing   15, 34
Provision for 'under-fives'   56–61

Safety in the home   69
Sensori-motor period   31
Social: relationship   ix, 19–26
       development   15, 17
Socialisation skills   15, 17–26

Time factor   ix, xiii

Wooden toys   37–43